THE EDINBURGH and DORÉ LECTURES

Other Books by Thomas Troward

THE HIDDEN POWER

THE LAW AND THE WORD

BIBLE MYSTERY AND BIBLE MEANING

THE CREATIVE PROCESS IN THE INDIVIDUAL

THOMAS TROWARD

THE EDINBURGH and DORÉ LECTURES

On Mental Science

Fides et Amor Veritas et Robur

DeVorss Publications
Camarillo, California

ISBN: 978-087516-614-8

DeVorss & Company, Publisher
P.O. Box 1389
Camarillo CA 93011-1389
www.devorss.com

Printed in the United States of America

CONTENTS

THE DORÉ LECTURES ON MENTAL SCIENCE

A WORD FROM THE PUBLISHER

THOMAS TROWARD (1847-1916) was Her Majesty's Assistant Commissioner and later Divisional Judge of the North Indian Punjab from 1869 until his retirement in 1896. It is this latter period for which he is best remembered and most celebrated; in it he was at last able to devote himself to his great interest in metaphysical and esoteric studies. The most notable result was a few small volumes that have had a profound effect on the development of spiritual metaphysics, in particular that of the New Thought movement, of which the teaching known as Science of Mind is Troward's most direct legacy.

Troward formally inaugurated his most important contribution to the New Thought philosophy with a series of lectures delivered in 1904 at Queen Street in Edinburgh. Published in the same year as *The Edinburgh Lectures on Mental Science*, they are the cornerstone of his philosophy and a milestone in the development of metaphysics, as well as the most comprehensive and concise statement of his teaching. William James, the American psychologist and philosopher whose famed *Varieties of Religious Experience* had also been a series of lectures delivered in Edinburgh only some two and a half years earlier, considered Troward's book "far and away the ablest statement of the philosophy that I have ever met, beautiful in its sustained clearness of thought and style; a really classic statement."

In 1909, Troward added three final chapters to his *Edinburgh Lectures* after having first clarified, reinforced, and amplified his earlier themes in a new series of lectures given at the Doré Art Gallery in London's fashionable Bond Street. These, published later in the year as *The Doré Lectures on Mental Science*, "flesh out" the more skeletal *Edinburgh Lectures* and suggest lines along which the reader can apply its principles. As such, *The Doré Lectures* is a splendid companion to, and complement of, the earlier work.

DeVorss & Company is proud to offer these two classics for the first time in a single volume. Together they present a scope of thought and reflection ranging from brilliant abstract reasoning to pastoral solicitude* for the reader's responsibility as a center of the creative process of the Universe itself. It was in the service of this concern that Troward labored with a distinction that endures to our own day—a distinction aptly characterized by the Latin device he so much favored, *Fides et Amor Veritas et Robur*: Faith and Love; Truth and Strength.

ARTHUR VERGARA
Editor

*See, for example, p. 87, line 20, to the bottom of p. 91; also ch. 10 of *The Doré Lectures*.

Notes, keyed to pages and lines of the text, appear on pp. 207–212.

THE EDINBURGH LECTURES ON MENTAL SCIENCE

THE WRITER
AFFECTIONATELY DEDICATES
THIS LITTLE VOLUME
TO
HIS WIFE

FOREWORD

This book contains the substance of a course of lectures recently given by the writer in the Queen Street Hall, Edinburgh. Its purpose is to indicate the *Natural Principles* governing the relation between Mental Action and Material Conditions, and thus to afford the student an intelligible starting point for the practical study of the subject.

T. T.

March 1904

1

SPIRIT AND MATTER

IN COMMENCING a course of lectures on Mental Science, it is somewhat difficult for the lecturer to fix upon the best method of opening the subject. It can be approached from many sides, each with some peculiar advantage of its own; but, after careful deliberation, it appears to me that, for the purpose of the present course, no better starting point could be selected than the relation between Spirit and Matter. I select this starting point because the distinction—or what we believe to be such—between them is one with which we are so familiar that I can safely assume its recognition by everybody; and I may, therefore, at once state this distinction by using the adjectives which we habitually apply as expressing the natural opposition between the two—*living* spirit and *dead* matter. These terms express our current impression of the opposition between spirit and matter with sufficient accuracy, and considered only from the point of view of outward appearances this impression is no doubt correct. The general consensus of mankind is right in trusting the evidence of our senses, and any system which tells us that we are not to do so will never obtain a permanent footing in a sane and healthy community. There is nothing wrong in the evidence conveyed to a healthy mind by the senses of a healthy body, but the point where error creeps in is when we come to judge of the meaning of this testimony. We are accustomed to judge only by external appearances and by certain limited significances which we attach to words; but when we begin to enquire into the real meaning of our words and to analyse the causes which give rise to the appearances, we find our old notions gradually falling off from us, until at last we wake up to the fact that we are living in an entirely different world to that we formerly recognized. The old limited mode of thought has imperceptibly slipped away, and we discover that we have stepped out into a new order of things where all is liberty and life. This is the work of an enlightened intelligence resulting from persistent determination to discover what truth really is irrespective of any preconceived notions from whatever source derived, the determination to think honestly for ourselves instead of endeavouring to get our thinking done for us. Let us then commence by enquiring what we really mean by the livingness which we attribute to spirit and the deadness which we attribute to matter.

At first we may be disposed to say that livingness consists in the power of motion and deadness in its absence; but a little enquiry into the most recent researches of science will soon show us that this distinction does not go deep enough. It is now one of the fully established facts of physical science that no atom of what we call "dead matter" is without motion. On the table before me lies a solid lump of steel, but in the light of up-to-date science I know that the atoms of that seemingly inert mass are vibrating with the most intense energy, continually dashing hither and thither, impinging upon and rebounding from one another, or circling round like miniature solar systems, with a ceaseless rapidity whose complex activity is enough to bewilder the imagination. The mass, as a mass, may lie inert upon the table; but so far from being destitute of the element of motion it is the abode of the never-tiring energy moving the particles with a swiftness to which the speed of an express train is as nothing. It is, therefore, not the mere fact of motion that is at the root of the distinction which we draw instinctively between spirit and matter; we must go deeper than that. The solution of the problem will never be found by comparing Life with what we call deadness, and the reason for this will become apparent later on; but the true key is to be found by comparing one degree of livingness with another. There is, of course, one sense in which the quality of livingness does not admit of degrees; but there is another sense in which it is entirely a question of degree. We have no doubt as to the livingness of a plant, but we realize that it is something very different from the livingness of an animal. Again, what average boy would not prefer a fox-terrier to a goldfish for a pet? Or, again, why is it that the boy himself is an advance upon the dog? The plant, the fish, the dog, and the boy are all equally *alive*; but there is a difference in the quality of their livingness about which no one can have any doubt, and no one would hesitate to say that this difference is in the degree of intelligence. In whatever way we turn the subject we shall always find that what we call the "livingness" of any individual life is ultimately measured by its intelligence. It is the possession of greater intelligence that places the animal higher in the scale of being than the plant, the man higher than the animal, the intellectual man higher than the savage. The increased intelligence calls into activity modes of motion of a higher order corresponding to itself. The higher the intelligence, the more completely the mode of motion is under its control; and as we descend in the scale of intelligence, the descent is marked by a corresponding increase in *automatic* motion not subject to the control of a self-conscious intelligence. This descent is gradual from the expanded self-recognition of the highest human personality to that lowest order of visible forms which we speak of as "things," and from which self-recognition is entirely absent.

We see, then, that the livingness of Life consists in intelligence—in other words, in the power of Thought; and we may therefore say that the distinctive quality of spirit is Thought, and, as the opposite to this, we may say that the distinctive quality of matter is Form. We cannot conceive of matter without form. Some form there must be, even though invisible to the physical eye; for matter, to be matter at all, must occupy space, and to occupy any particular space necessarily implies a corresponding form. For these reasons we may lay it down as a fundamental proposition that the distinctive quality of spirit is Thought and the distinctive quality of matter is Form. This is a radical distinction from which important consequences follow, and should, therefore, be carefully noted by the student.

Form implies extension in space and also limitation

within certain boundaries. Thought implies neither. When, therefore, we think of Life as existing in any particular *form* we associate it with the idea of extension in space, so that an elephant may be said to consist of a vastly larger amount of living substance than a mouse. But if we think of Life as the fact of livingness we do not associate it with any idea of extension, and we at once realize that the mouse is quite as much alive as the elephant, notwithstanding the difference in size. The important point of this distinction is that if we can conceive of anything as entirely devoid of the element of extension in space, it must be present in its entire totality anywhere and everywhere—that is to say, at every point of space simultaneously. The scientific definition of time is that it is the period occupied by a body in passing from one given point in space to another, and, therefore, according to this definition, when there is no space there can be no time; and hence that conception of spirit which realizes it as devoid of the element of space must realize it as being devoid of the element of time also; and we therefore find that the conception of spirit as pure Thought, and not as concrete Form, is the conception of it as subsisting perfectly independently of the elements of time and space. From this it follows that if the idea of anything is conceived as existing on this level it can only represent that thing as being actually present here and now. In this view of things nothing can be remote from us either in time or space: either the idea is entirely dissipated or it exists as an actual present entity, and not as something that *shall* be in the future, for where there is no sequence in time there can be no future. Similarly where there is no space there can be no conception of anything as being at a distance from us. When the elements of time and space are eliminated all our ideas of things must necessarily be as subsisting in a universal here and an everlasting now. This is, no doubt, a highly abstract conception, but I would ask the student to endeavour to grasp it thoroughly, since it is of vital importance in the practical application of Mental Science, as will appear further on.

The opposite conception is that of things expressing themselves through conditions of time and space and thus establishing a variety of *relations* to other things, as of bulk, distance, and direction, or of sequence in time. These two conceptions are respectively the conception of the abstract and the concrete, of the unconditioned and the conditioned, of the absolute and the relative. They are not opposed to each other in the sense of incompatibility, but are each the complement of the other, and the only reality is in the combination of the two. The error of the extreme idealist is in endeavouring to realize the absolute without the relative, and the error of the extreme materialist is in endeavouring to realize the relative without the absolute. On the one side the mistake is in trying to realize an inside without an outside, and on the other in trying to realize an outside without an inside; both are necessary to the formation of a substantial entity.

2

THE HIGHER MODE OF INTELLIGENCE CONTROLS THE LOWER

WE HAVE SEEN that the descent from personality, as we know it in ourselves, to matter, as we know it under what we call inanimate forms, is a gradual descent in the scale of intelligence from that mode of being which is able to realize its own will-power as a capacity for originating new trains of causation to that mode of being which is incapable of recognizing itself at all. The higher the grade of life, the higher the intelligence; from which it follows that the supreme principle of Life must also be the ultimate principle of intelligence. This is clearly demonstrated by the grand natural order of the universe. In the light of modern science the principle of evolution is familiar to us all, and the accurate adjustment existing between all parts of the cosmic scheme is too self-evident to need insisting upon. Every advance in science consists in discovering new subtleties of connection in this magnificent universal order, which already exists and only needs our recognition to bring it into practical use. If, then, the highest work of the greatest minds consists in nothing else than the recognition of an already existing order, there is no getting away from the conclusion that a paramount intelligence must be inherent in the Life-Principle, which manifests itself *as* this order; and thus we see that there must be a great cosmic intelligence underlying the totality of things.

The physical history of our planet shows us first an incandescent nebula dispersed over vast infinitudes of space; later this condenses into a central sun surrounded by a family of glowing planets hardly yet consolidated from the plastic primordial matter; then succeed untold millenniums of slow geological formation; an earth peopled by the lowest forms of life, whether vegetable or animal; from which crude beginnings a majestic, unceasing, unhurried, forward movement brings things stage by stage to the condition in which we know them now. Looking at this steady progression it is clear that, however we may conceive the nature of the evolutionary principle, it unerringly provides for the continual advance of the race. But it does this by creating such numbers of each kind that, after allowing a wide margin for all possible accidents to individuals, the race shall still continue:

> So careful of the type it seems,
> So careless of the single life.

In short, we may say that the cosmic intelligence works by a Law of Averages which allows a wide margin of accident and failure to the individual.

But the progress towards higher intelligence is always in the direction of narrowing down this margin of accident and taking the individual more and more out of the law of averages, and substituting the law of individual selection. In ordinary scientific language this is the survival of the fittest. The reproduction of fish is on a scale that would choke the sea with them if every individual survived; but the margin of destruction is correspondingly enormous, and thus the law of averages simply keeps up the normal proportion of the race. But at the other end of the scale, reproduction is by no means thus enormously in excess of survival. True, there is ample margin of accident and disease cutting off numbers of human beings before they have gone through the average duration of life, but still it is on a very different scale from the premature destruction of hundreds of thousands as against the survival of one. It may, therefore, be taken as an established fact that in proportion as intelligence advances, the individual ceases to be subject to a mere law of averages and has a continually increasing power of controlling the conditions of his own survival.

We see, therefore, that there is a marked distinction between the cosmic intelligence and the individual intelligence, and that the factor which differentiates the latter from the former is the presence of *individual* volition. Now the business of Mental Science is to ascertain the relation of this individual power of volition to the great cosmic law which provides for the maintenance and advancement of the race; and the point to be carefully noted is that the power of individual volition is itself the outcome of the cosmic evolutionary principle at the point where it reaches its highest level. The effort of Nature has always been upwards from the time when only the lowest forms of life peopled the globe, and it has now culminated in the production of a being with a mind capable of abstract reasoning and a brain fitted to be the physical instrument of such a mind. At this stage the all-creating Life-principle reproduces itself in a form capable of recognizing the working of the evolutionary law, and the unity and continuity of purpose running through the whole progression until now indicates, beyond a doubt, that the place of such a being in the universal scheme must be to introduce the operation of that factor which, up to this point, has been conspicuous by its absence—the factor, namely, of intelligent individual volition. The evolution which has brought us up to this standpoint has worked by a cosmic law of averages; it has been a process in which the individual himself has not taken a conscious part. But because he is what he is, and leads the van of the evolutionary procession, if man is to evolve further, it can now only be by his own conscious cooperation with the law which has brought him up to the standpoint where he is able to realize that such a law exists. His evolution in the future must be by conscious participation in the great work, and this can only be effected by his own individual intelligence and effort. It is a process of intelligent growth. No one else can grow for us; we must each grow for ourselves; and this intelligent growth consists in our increasing recognition of the universal law, which has brought us as far as we have yet got, and of our own individual relation to that law, based upon the fact that we ourselves are the most advanced product of it. It is a great maxim that Nature obeys us precisely in proportion as we first obey Nature. Let the electrician try to go counter to the principle that electricity must always pass from a higher to a lower potential and he will effect nothing; but let him submit in all things to this one fundamental law, and he can make whatever particular applications of electrical power he will.

These considerations show us that what differentiates the higher from the lower degree of intelligence is the recognition of its own self-hood, and the more intelligent that recognition is, the greater will be the power. The lower degree of self-recognition is that which only realizes itself as an entity separate from all other entities, as the *ego* distinguished from the *non-ego*. But the higher degree of self-recognition is that which, realizing its own spiritual nature, sees in all other forms, not so much the *non-ego*, or that which is not itself, as the *alter-ego*, or that which is itself in a different mode of expression. Now, it is this higher degree of self-recognition that is the power by which the Mental Scientist produces his results. For this reason it is imperative that he should clearly understand the difference between Form and Being; that the one is the mode of the relative and the mark of subjection to conditions, and that the other is the truth of the absolute and is that which controls conditions.

Now this higher recognition of self as an individualization of pure spirit must of necessity control all modes of spirit which have not yet reached the same level of self-recognition. These lower modes of spirit are in bondage to the law of their own being because they do not know the law; and, therefore, the individual who has attained to this knowledge can control them through that law. But to understand this we must enquire a little further into the nature of spirit. I have already shown that the grand scale of adaptation and adjustment of all parts of the cosmic scheme to one another exhibits the presence *somewhere* of a marvellous intelligence underlying the whole, and the question is, where is this intelligence to be found? Ultimately we can only conceive of it as inherent in some primordial substance which is the root of all those grosser modes of matter which are known to us, whether visible to the physical eye, or necessarily inferred by science from their perceptible effects. It is that power which, in every species and in every individual, becomes that which that species or individual is; and thus we can only conceive of it as a self-forming intelligence inherent in the ultimate substance of which each thing is a particular manifestation. That this primordial substance must be considered as self-forming by an inherent intelligence abiding in itself becomes evident from the fact that intelligence is the essential quality of spirit; and if we were to conceive of the primordial substance as something apart from spirit, then we should have to postulate some other power which is neither spirit nor matter, and originates both; but this is only putting the idea of a self-evolving power a step further back and asserting the production of a lower grade of undifferentiated spirit by a higher, which is both a purely gratuitous assumption and a contradiction of any idea we can form of undifferentiated spirit at all. However far back, therefore, we may relegate the original starting point, we cannot avoid the conclusion that, at that point, spirit contains the primary substance in itself, which brings us back to the common statement that it made everything out of nothing. We thus find two factors to the making of all things, Spirit and—

Nothing; and the addition of Nothing to Spirit leaves *only* spirit: $x + o = x$.

From these considerations we see that the ultimate foundation of every form of matter is spirit, and hence that a universal intelligence subsists throughout Nature inherent in every one of its manifestations. But this cryptic intelligence does not belong to the particular *form* excepting in the measure in which it is physically fitted for its concentration into self-recognizing individuality: it lies hidden in that primordial substance of which the visible form is a grosser manifestation. This primordial substance is a philosophical necessity, and we can only picture it to ourselves as something infinitely finer than the atoms which are themselves a philosophical inference of physical science: still, for want of a better word, we may conveniently speak of this primary intelligence inherent in the very substance of things as the Atomic Intelligence. The term may, perhaps, be open to some objections, but it will serve our present purpose as distinguishing *this* mode of spirit's intelligence from that of the opposite pole, or Individual Intelligence. This distinction should be carefully noted because it is by the response of the atomic intelligence to the individual intelligence that thought-power is able to produce results on the material plane, as in the cure of disease by mental treatment, and the like. Intelligence manifests itself by responsiveness, and the whole action of the cosmic mind in bringing the evolutionary process from its first beginnings up to its present human stage is nothing else but a continual intelligent response to the demand which each stage in the progress has made for an adjustment between itself and its environment. Since, then, we have recognized the presence of a universal intelligence permeating all things, we must also recognize a corresponding responsiveness hidden deep down in their nature and ready to be called into action when appealed to. All mental treatment depends on this responsiveness of spirit in its lower degrees to higher degrees of itself. It is here that the difference between the mental scientist and the uninstructed person comes in; the former knows of this responsiveness and makes use of it, and the latter cannot use it because he does not know it.

3

THE UNITY OF THE SPIRIT

We have now paved the way for understanding what is meant by "the unity of the spirit." In the first conception of spirit as the underlying origin of all things we see a universal substance which, at this stage, is not differentiated into any specific forms. This is not a question of some bygone time, but subsists at every moment of all time in the *innermost* nature of all being; and when we see this, we see that the division between one specific form and another has below it a deep essential unity, which acts as the supporter of all the several forms of individuality arising out of it. And as our thought penetrates deeper into the nature of this all-producing spiritual substance we see that it cannot be limited to any one portion of space, but must be limitless as space itself, and that the idea of any portion of space where it is not is inconceivable. It is one of those intuitive perceptions from which the human mind can never get away that this primordial, all-generating living spirit must be commensurate with infinitude, and we can therefore never think of it otherwise than as universal or infinite. Now it is a mathematical truth that the infinite must be a unity.

You cannot have two infinites, for then neither would be infinite, each would be limited by the other; nor can you split the infinite up into fractions. The infinite is mathematically essential unity. This is a point on which too much stress cannot be laid, for there follow from it the most important consequences. Unity, as such, can be neither multiplied nor divided, for either operation destroys the unity. By multiplying, we produce a plurality of units of the same scale as the original; and by dividing, we produce a plurality of units of a smaller scale; and a plurality of units is not unity but multiplicity. Therefore if we would penetrate below the outward nature of the individual to that innermost principle of his being from which his individuality takes its rise, we can do so only by passing beyond the conception of individual existence into that of the unity of universal being. This may appear to be a merely philosophical abstraction, but the student who would produce practical results must realize that these abstract generalizations are the foundation of the practical work he is going to do.

Now the great fact to be recognized about a unity is that, *because* it is a single unit, wherever it is at all the *whole* of it must be. The moment we allow our mind to wander off to the idea of extension in space and say that one part of the unit is here and another there, we have descended from the idea of unity into that of parts or fractions of a single unit, which is to pass into the idea of a multiplicity of smaller units, and in that case we are dealing with the relative, or the relation subsisting between two or more entities which are therefore *limited by each other*, and so have passed out of the region of simple unity which is the absolute. It is, therefore, a mathematical necessity that, because the originating Life-principle is infinite, it is a single unit, and consequently, wherever it is at all, the *whole* of it must be present. But because it is *infinite*, or limitless, it is everywhere, and therefore it follows that the *whole* of spirit must be present at every point in space at the same moment. Spirit is thus omnipresent *in its entirety*, and it is accordingly logically correct that at every moment of time *all* spirit is concentrated at any point in space that we may choose to fix our thought upon. This is the fundamental fact of all being, and it is for this reason that I have prepared the way for it by laying down the relation between spirit and matter as that between idea and form, on the one hand the absolute from which the elements of time and space are entirely absent, and on the other the relative which is entirely dependent on those elements. This great fact is that pure spirit continually subsists in the absolute, whether in a corporeal body or not; and from it all the phenomena of being flow, whether on the mental plane or the physical. The knowledge of this fact regarding spirit is the basis of all conscious spiritual operation, and therefore in proportion to our increasing recognition of it our power of producing outward visible results by the action of our thought will grow. The whole is greater than its part, and therefore, if, by our recognition of this unity, we can concentrate *all* spirit into any given point at any moment, we thereby include any individualization of it that we may wish to deal with. The practical importance of this conclusion is too obvious to need enlarging upon.

Pure spirit is the Life-principle considered apart

from the matrix in which it takes relation to time and space in a particular form. In this aspect it is pure intelligence undifferentiated into individuality. As pure intelligence it is infinite responsiveness and susceptibility. As devoid of relation to time and space it is devoid of individual personality. It is, therefore, in this aspect a purely impersonal element upon which, by reason of its inherent intelligence and susceptibility, we can impress any recognition of personality that we will. These are the great facts that the mental scientist works with, and the student will do well to ponder deeply on their significance and on the responsibilities which their realization must necessarily carry with it.

4

SUBJECTIVE AND OBJECTIVE MIND

Up to this point it has been necessary to lay the foundations of the science by the statement of highly abstract general principles which we have reached by purely metaphysical reasoning. We now pass on to the consideration of certain natural laws which have been established by a long series of experiments and observations, the full meaning and importance of which will become clear when we see their application to the general principles which have hitherto occupied our attention. The phenomena of hypnosis are now so fully recognized as established scientific facts that it is quite superfluous to discuss the question of their credibility. Two great medical schools have been founded upon them, and in some countries they have become the subject of special legislation. The question before us at the present day is, not as to the credibility of the facts, but as to the proper inferences to be drawn from them, and a correct apprehension of these inferences is one of the most valuable aids to the mental scientist, for it confirms the conclusions of purely *a priori* reasoning by an array of experimental instances which places the correctness of those conclusions beyond doubt.

The great truth which the science of hypnotism has brought to light is the dual nature of the human mind. Much conflict exists between different writers as to whether this duality results from the presence of two actually separate minds in the one man, or in the action of the same mind in the employment of different functions. This is one of those distinctions without a difference which are so prolific a source of hindrance to the opening out of truth. A man must be a single individuality to be a man at all, and so the net result is the same whether we conceive of his varied modes of mental action as proceeding from a set of separate minds strung, so to speak, on the thread of his one individuality and each adapted to a particular use, or as varied functions of a single mind; in either case we are dealing with a single individuality, and how we may picture the wheel-work of the mental mechanism is merely a question of what picture will bring the nature of its action home to us most clearly. Therefore, as a matter of convenience, I shall in these lectures speak of this dual action as though it proceeded from two minds, an outer and an inner, and the inner mind we will call the subjective mind and the outer the objective, by which names the distinction is most frequently indicated in the literature of the subject.

A long series of careful experiments by highly trained observers, some of them men of worldwide reputation, has fully established certain remarkable differences between the action of the subjective and that of the objective mind which may be briefly stated as follows. The subjective mind is only able to reason *deductively* and not inductively, while the objective mind can do both. Deductive reasoning is the pure syllogism which shows why a third proposition must necessarily result if two others are assumed, but which does not help us to determine whether the two initial statements are true or not. To determine this is the province of inductive reasoning which draws its conclusions from the observation of a series of facts. The relation of the two modes of reasoning is that, first by observing a sufficient number of instances, we inductively reach the conclusion that a certain principle is of general application, and then we enter upon the deductive process by assuming the truth of this principle and determining what result must follow in a particular case on the hypothesis of its truth. Thus deductive reasoning proceeds on the assumption of the correctness of certain hypotheses or suppositions with which it sets out; it is not concerned with the truth or falsity of those suppositions, but only with the question as to what results must necessarily follow supposing them to be true. Inductive reasoning, on the other hand, is the process by which we compare a number of separate instances with one another until we see the common factor that gives rise to them all. Induction proceeds by the comparison of facts, and deduction by the application of universal principles. Now it is the deductive method only which is followed by the subjective mind. Innumerable experiments on persons in the hypnotic state have shown that the subjective mind is utterly incapable of making the selection and comparison which are necessary to the inductive process, but will accept any suggestion, however false, but having once accepted any suggestion, it is strictly logical in deducing the proper conclusions from it, and works out every suggestion to the minutest fraction of the results which flow from it.

As a consequence of this it follows that the subjective mind is entirely under the control of the objective mind. With the utmost fidelity it reproduces and works out to its final consequences whatever the objective mind impresses upon it; and the facts of hypnotism show that ideas can be impressed on the subjective mind by the objective mind of another as well as by that of its own individuality. This is a most important point, for it is on this amenability to suggestion by the thought of another that all the phenomena of healing, whether present or absent, of telepathy and the like, depend. Under the control of the practised hypnotist the very personality of the subject becomes changed for the time being; he believes himself to be whatever the operator tells him he is: he is a swimmer breasting the waves, a bird flying in the air, a soldier in the tumult of battle, an Indian stealthily tracking his victim; in short, for the time being, he identifies himself with any personality that is impressed upon him by the will of the operator, and acts the part with inimitable accuracy. But the experiments of hypnotism go further than this, and show the existence in the subjective mind of powers far transcending any exercised by the objective mind through the medium of the physical senses; powers of thought-reading, of thought-transference, of clairvoyance, and the like, all of which are frequently manifested when the patient is brought into the higher mesmeric state; and we have thus experimental proof of the existence in ourselves of transcendental faculties the full development and conscious control of which would place us in a perfectly new sphere of life.

But it should be noted that the control must be *our own* and not that of any external intelligence whether in the flesh or out of it.

But perhaps the most important fact which hypnotic experiments have demonstrated is that the subjective mind is the builder of the body. The subjective entity in the patient is able to diagnose the character of the disease from which he is suffering and to point out suitable remedies, indicating a physiological knowledge exceeding that of the most highly trained physicians, and also a knowledge of the correspondences between diseased conditions of the bodily organs and the material remedies which can afford relief. And from this it is but a step further to those numerous instances in which it entirely dispenses with the use of material remedies and itself works directly on the organism, so that complete restoration to health follows as the result of the suggestions of perfect soundness made by the operator to the patient while in the hypnotic state.

Now these are facts fully established by hundreds of experiments conducted by a variety of investigators in different parts of the world, and from them we may draw two inferences of the highest importance: one, that the subjective mind is in itself absolutely impersonal, and the other that it is the builder of the body, or in other words it is the creative power in the individual. That it is impersonal in itself is shown by its readiness to assume any personality the hypnotist chooses to impress upon it; and the unavoidable inference is that its realization of personality proceeds from its association with the particular objective mind of its own individuality. Whatever personality the objective mind impresses upon it, that personality it assumes and acts up to; and since it is the builder of the body, it will build up a body in correspondence with the personality thus impressed upon it. These two laws of the subjective mind form the foundation of the axiom that our body represents the aggregate of our beliefs. If our fixed belief is that the body is subject to all sorts of influences beyond our control, and that this, that, or the other symptom shows that such an uncontrollable influence is at work upon us, then this belief is impressed upon the subjective mind, which by the law of its nature accepts it without question and proceeds to fashion bodily conditions in accordance with this belief. Again, if our fixed belief is that certain material remedies are the only means of cure, then we find in this belief the foundation of all medicine. There is nothing unsound in the theory of medicine; it is the strictly logical correspondence with the measure of knowledge which those who rely on it are as yet able to assimilate, and it acts accurately in accordance with their belief that in a large number of cases medicine will do good, but also in many instances it fails. Therefore, for those who have not yet reached a more interior perception of the law of Nature, the healing agency of medicine is a most valuable aid to the alleviation of physical maladies. The error to be combated is not the belief that, in its own way, medicine is capable of doing good, but the belief that there is no higher or better way.

Then, on the same principle, if we realize that the subjective mind is the builder of the body, and that the body is subject to no influences except those which reach it through the subjective mind, then what we have to do is to impress *this* upon the subjective mind and habitually think of it as a fountain of perpetual Life, which is continually renovating the body by building in strong and healthy material, in the most complete independence of any influences of any sort, save those of our own desire impressed upon our own subjective mind by our own thought. When once we fully grasp these considerations we shall see that it is just as easy to externalize healthy conditions of body as the contrary. Practically the process amounts to a belief in our own power of life; and since this belief, if it be thoroughly domiciled within us, will necessarily produce a correspondingly healthy body, we should spare no pains to convince ourselves that there are sound and reasonable grounds for holding it. To afford a solid basis for this conviction is the purpose of Mental Science.

5

FURTHER CONSIDERATIONS REGARDING SUBJECTIVE AND OBJECTIVE MIND

An intelligent consideration of the phenomena of hypnotism will show us that what we call the hypnotic state is the *normal* state of the subjective mind. It *always* conceives of itself in accordance with some suggestion conveyed to it, either consciously or unconsciously to the mode of objective mind which governs it, and it gives rise to corresponding external results. The abnormal nature of the conditions induced by experimental hypnotism is in the removal of the normal control held by the individual's own objective mind over his subjective mind and the substitution of some other control for it, and thus we may say that the normal characteristic of the subjective mind is its perpetual action in accordance with some sort of suggestion. It becomes therefore a question of the highest importance to determine in every case what the nature of the suggestion shall be and from what source it shall proceed; but before considering the sources of suggestion we must realize more fully the place taken by subjective mind in the order of Nature.

If the student has followed what has been said regarding the presence of intelligent spirit pervading all space and permeating all matter, he will now have little difficulty in recognizing this all-pervading spirit as universal subjective mind. That it cannot *as universal mind* have the qualities of objective mind is very obvious. The universal mind is the creative power throughout Nature; and as the originating power it must first give rise to the various *forms* in which objective mind recognizes its own individuality, before these individual minds can react upon it; and hence, as pure spirit or *first cause*, it cannot possibly be anything else than subjective mind; and the fact, which has been abundantly proved by experiment, that the subjective mind is the builder of the body shows us that the power of creating by growth from within is the essential characteristic of the subjective mind. Hence, both from experiment and from *a priori* reasoning, we may say that wherever we find creative power at work, there we are in the presence of subjective mind, whether it be working on the grand scale of the cosmos, or on the miniature scale of the individual. We may therefore lay it down as a principle that the universal all-permeating intelligence, which has been considered in the second and third sections, is purely subjective mind, and therefore follows the law of subjective mind, namely that it is amenable to any suggestion, and will carry out any suggestion that is impressed upon it to its most rigorously logical consequences. The incalculable importance of this truth may not perhaps strike the student at first sight, but a little consideration will show him the enormous possibilities that are stored up in it, and in the concluding section I shall briefly touch upon the very serious conclusions resulting from it. For the present it will be sufficient to realize that the subjective mind in ourselves is *the same* subjective mind which is at work throughout the universe giving rise to the infinitude of natural forms with which we are surrounded, and in like manner giving rise *to ourselves also*. It may be called the supporter of our individuality; and we may loosely speak of our individual subjective mind as our personal share in the universal mind. This, of course, does not imply the splitting up of the universal mind into fractions, and it is to avoid this error that I have discussed the essential unity of spirit in the third section; but in order to avoid too highly abstract conceptions in the present stage of the student's progress, we may conveniently employ the idea of a personal share in the universal subjective mind.

To realize our individual subjective mind in this manner will help us to get over the great metaphysical difficulty which meets us in our endeavour to make conscious use of first cause, in other words to create external results by the power of our own thought. Ultimately there can be only one first cause which is the universal mind, but because it is universal it cannot, *as universal*, act on the plane of the individual and particular. For it to do so would be for it to cease to be universal and therefore cease to be the creative power which we wish to employ. On the other hand, the fact that we are working for a specific definite object implies our intention to use this universal power in application to a particular purpose, and thus we find ourselves involved in the paradox of seeking to make the universal act on the plane of the particular. We want to effect a junction between the two extremes of the scale of Nature, the innermost creative spirit and a particular external form. Between these two is a great gulf, and the question is how it is to be bridged over. It is here, then, that the conception of our individual subjective mind as our personal share in the universal subjective mind affords the means of meeting the difficulty, for on the one hand it is in immediate connection with the universal mind, and on the other it is in immediate connection with the individual objective, or intellectual mind; and this in its turn is in immediate connection with the world of externalization, which is conditioned in time and space; and thus the relation between the subjective and objective minds in the individual forms the bridge which is needed to connect the two extremities of the scale.

The individual subjective mind may therefore be regarded as the organ of the Absolute in precisely the same way that the objective mind is the organ of the Relative, and it is in order to regulate our use of these two organs that it is necessary to understand what the terms "absolute" and "relative" actually mean. The absolute is that idea of a thing which contemplates it as existing *in itself* and not in relation to something else, that is to say, which contemplates the essence of it; and the relative is that idea of a thing which contemplates it as related to other things, that is to say as circumscribed by a certain environment. The absolute is the region of causes, and the relative is the region of conditions; and hence, if we wish to control conditions, this can only be done by our thought-power operating on the plane of the absolute, which it can do only through the medium of the subjective mind. The conscious use of the creative power of thought consists in the attainment of the power of Thinking in the Absolute, and this can only be attained by a clear conception of the interaction between our different mental functions. For this purpose the student cannot too strongly impress upon himself that subjective mind, on whatever scale, is intensely sensitive to suggestion, and as creative power works accurately to the externalization of that suggestion which is most deeply impressed upon it. If then, we would take any idea out of the realm of the relative, where it is limited and restricted by conditions imposed upon it through surrounding circumstances, and transfer it to the realm of the absolute where it is not thus limited, a right recognition of our mental constitution will enable us to do this by a clearly defined method.

The object of our desire is necessarily first conceived by us as bearing some relation to existing circumstances, which may, or may not, appear favourable to it; and what we want to do is to eliminate the element of contingency and attain something which is certain in itself. To do this is to work upon the plane of the absolute, and for this purpose we must endeavour to impress upon our subjective mind the idea of that which we desire quite apart from any conditions. This separation from the elements of condition implies the elimination of the idea of *time*, and consequently we must think of the thing as already in actual existence. Unless we do this we are not consciously operating upon the plane of the absolute, and are therefore not employing the creative power of our thought. The simplest practical method of gaining the habit of thinking in this manner is to conceive the existence in the spiritual world of a spiritual prototype of every existing thing, which becomes the root of the corresponding external existence. If we thus habituate ourselves to look on the spiritual prototype as the essential being of the thing, and the material form as the growth of this prototype into outward expression, then we shall see that the initial step to the production of any external fact must be the creation of its spiritual prototype. This prototype, being purely spiritual, can only be formed by the operation of *thought*, and in order to have substance on the spiritual plane it *must* be thought of as actually existing there. This conception has been elaborated by Plato in his doctrine of archetypal ideas, and by Swedenborg in his doctrine of correspondences; and a still greater teacher has said "All things whatsoever ye pray and ask for, believe that ye *have* received them, and ye *shall* receive them" (Mark 11: 24, R.V.). The difference of the tenses in this passage is remarkable. The speaker bids us first to believe that our desire *has* already been fulfilled, that it is a thing already accomplished, and then its accomplishment *will* follow as a thing in the future. This is nothing else than a concise direction for making use of the creative power of thought by impressing upon the universal subjective mind the particular thing which we desire as an already existing fact. In following this direction we are thinking on the plane of the absolute and eliminating from our minds all consideration of conditions, which imply limitation and the possibility of adverse contingencies; and we are thus planting a seed which, if left undisturbed, will infallibly germinate into external fruition.

By thus making intelligent use of our subjective mind, we, so to speak, create a *nucleus*, which is no sooner created than it begins to exercise an attractive force, drawing to itself material of a like character with its own, and if this process is allowed to go on undisturbed, it will continue until an external form corresponding to the nature of the nucleus comes out into manifestation on the plane of the objective and relative. This is the universal method of Nature on every plane. Some of the most advanced thinkers in modern physical science, in the endeavour to probe the great mystery of the first origin of the world, have postulated the formation of what they call "vortex rings" formed from an infinitely fine primordial substance. They tell us that if such a ring be once formed on the minutest scale and set rotating, then, since it would be moving in pure ether and subject to no friction, it must according to all known laws of physics be indestructible and its motion perpetual. Let two such rings approach each other, and by the law of attraction, they would coalesce into a whole, and so on until manifested matter as we apprehend it with our external senses, is at last formed. Of course no one has ever seen these rings with the physical eye. They are one of those abstractions which result if we follow out the observed law of physics and the unavoidable sequences of mathematics to their necessary consequences. We cannot account for the things that we *can* see unless we assume the existence of other things which we *cannot*; and the "vortex theory" is one of these assumptions. This theory has not been put forward by mental scientists but by purely physical scientists as the ultimate conclusion to which their researches have led them, and this conclusion is that all the innumerable forms of Nature have their origin in the infinitely minute nucleus of the vortex ring, by whatever means the vortex ring may have received its initial impulse, a question with which physical science, as such, is not concerned.

As the vortex theory accounts for the formation of the inorganic world, so does biology account for the formation of the living organism. That also has its origin in a primary nucleus which, as soon as it is established, operates as a centre of attraction for the formation of all those physical organs of which the perfect individual is composed. The science of embryology shows that this rule holds good without exception throughout the whole range of the animal world, including man; and botany shows the same principle at work throughout the vegetable world. All branches of physical science demonstrate the fact that every completed manifestation, of whatever kind and on whatever scale, is started by the establishment of a nucleus, infinitely small but endowed with an unquenchable energy of attraction, causing it to steadily increase in power and definiteness of purpose, until the process of growth is completed and the matured form stands out as an accomplished fact. Now if this be the universal method of Nature, there is nothing unnatural in supposing that it must begin its operation at a stage further back than the formation of the material nucleus. As soon as that is called into being it begins to operate by the law of attraction on the material plane; but what is the force which originates the material nucleus? Let a recent work on physical science give us the answer; "In its ultimate essence, energy may be incomprehensible by us except as an exhibition of the direct operation of that which we call

Mind or Will." The quotation is from a course of lectures on "Waves in Water, Air and Æther," delivered in 1902, at the Royal Institution, by J. A. Fleming. Here, then, is the testimony of physical science that the originating energy is Mind or Will; and we are, therefore, not only making a logical deduction from certain unavoidable intuitions of the human mind, but are also following on the lines of the most advanced physical science, when we say that the action of Mind plants that nucleus which, if allowed to grow undisturbed, will eventually attract to itself all the conditions necessary for its manifestation in outward visible form. Now the only action of Mind is Thought; and it is for this reason that by our thoughts we create corresponding external conditions, because we thereby create the nucleus which attracts to itself its own correspondences in due order until the finished work is manifested on the external plane. This is according to the strictly scientific conception of the universal law of growth; and we may therefore briefly sum up the whole argument by saying that our thought of anything forms a spiritual prototype of it, thus constituting a nucleus or centre of attraction for all conditions necessary to its eventual externalization by a law of growth inherent in the prototype itself.

6

THE LAW OF GROWTH

A CORRECT understanding of the law of growth is of the highest importance to the student of Mental Science. The great fact to be realized regarding Nature is that it is natural. We may pervert the order of Nature, but it will prevail in the long run, returning, as Horace says, by the back door even though we drive it out with a pitchfork; and the beginning, the middle, and the end of the law of Nature is the principle of growth from a vitality inherent in the entity itself. If we realize this from the outset we shall not undo our own work by endeavouring to *force* things to become that which by their own nature they are not. For this reason when the Bible says that "he who believeth shall not make haste," it is enunciating a great natural principle that success depends on our using, and not opposing, the universal law of growth. No doubt the greater the vitality we put into the germ, which we have agreed to call the spiritual prototype, the quicker it will germinate; but this is simply because by a more realizing conception we put more growing-power into the seed than we do by a feebler conception. Our mistakes always eventually resolve themselves into distrusting the law of growth. Either we fancy we can hasten it by some exertion of our own from *without*, and are thus led into hurry and anxiety, not to say sometimes into the employment of grievously wrong methods; or else we give up all hope and so deny the germinating power of the seed we have planted. The result in either case is the same, for in either case we are in effect forming a fresh spiritual prototype of an opposite character to our desire, which therefore neutralizes the one first formed, and disintegrates it and usurps its place. The law is always the same, that our Thought forms a spiritual prototype which, if left undisturbed, will reproduce itself in external circumstances; the only difference is in the sort of prototype we form, and thus evil is brought to us by precisely the same law as good.

These considerations will greatly simplify our ideas of life. We have no longer to consider two forces, but only one, as being the cause of all things; the difference between good and evil resulting simply from the direction in which this force is made to flow. It is a universal law that if we reverse the action of a cause we at the same time reverse the effect. With the same apparatus we can commence by mechanical motion which will generate electricity, or we can commence with electricity which will generate mechanical motion; or to take a simple arithmetical instance: if $10 \div 2 = 5$, then $10 \div 5 = 2$; and therefore if we once recognize the power of thought to produce any results at all, we shall see that the law by which negative thought produces negative results is the same by which positive thought produces positive results. Therefore all our distrust of the law of growth, whether shown in the anxious endeavour to bring pressure to bear from without, or in allowing despair to take the place of cheerful expectation, is reversing the action of the original cause and consequently reversing the nature of the results. It is for this reason that the Bible, which is the most deeply occult of all books, continually lays so much stress upon the efficiency of faith and the destructive influence of unbelief; and in like manner, all books on every branch of spiritual science emphatically warn us against the admission of doubt or fear. They are the inversion of the principle which builds up, and they are therefore the principle which pulls down; but the Law itself never changes, and it is on the unchangeableness of the law that all Mental Science is founded. We are accustomed to realize the unchangeableness of natural law in our everyday life, and it should therefore not be difficult to realize that the same unchangeableness of law which obtains on the visible side of nature obtains on the invisible side as well. The variable factor is, not the law, but our own volition; and it is by combining this variable factor with the invariable one that we can produce the various results we desire. The principle of growth is that of inherent vitality in the seed itself, and the operations of the gardener have their exact analogue in Mental Science. We do not *put* the self-expansive vitality into the seed, but we must sow it, and we may also, so to speak, water it by quiet concentrated contemplation of our desire as an actually accomplished fact. But we must carefully remove from such contemplation any idea of a strenuous effort on our part to *make* the seed grow. Its efficacy is in helping to keep out those negative thoughts of doubt which would plant tares among our wheat, and therefore, instead of anything of effort, such contemplation should be accompanied by a feeling of pleasure and restfulness in foreseeing the certain accomplishment of our desires. This is that making our requests known to God *with thanksgiving* which St. Paul recommends, and it has its reason in that perfect wholeness of the Law of Being which only needs our recognition of it to be used by us to any extent we wish.

Some people possess the power of visualization, or making mental pictures of things, in a greater degree than others, and by such this faculty may advantageously be employed to facilitate their realization of the working of the Law. But those who do not possess this faculty in any marked degree, need not be discouraged by their want of it, for visualization is not the only way of realizing that the law is at work on the invisible plane. Those whose mental bias is towards physical science should realize this Law of Growth as the creative force throughout all nature; and those who have a mathematical turn of mind may reflect that all solids are generated from the movement of a point, which, as our old friend Euclid tells us, is that which has no parts nor magnitude, and is therefore as complete an abstraction as any spiritual nucleus could be. To use the apostolic words, we are dealing with the substance of things not seen, and we have to attain that habit of mind by which we shall see its reality and feel that we are mentally manipulating the only substance there ultimately is, and of which all visible things are only different modes. We must therefore regard our mental creations as spiritual realities and then implicitly trust the Law of Growth to do the rest.

7

RECEPTIVITY

IN ORDER to lay the foundations for practical work, the student must endeavour to get a clear conception of what is meant by the intelligence of undifferentiated spirit. We want to grasp the idea of intelligence apart from individuality, an idea which is rather apt to elude us until we grow accustomed to it. It is the failure to realize this quality of spirit that has given rise to all the theological errors that have brought bitterness into the world and has been prominent amongst the causes which have retarded the true development of mankind. To accurately convey this conception in words, is perhaps, impossible, and to attempt definition is to introduce that very idea of limitation which is our object to avoid. It is a matter of feeling rather than of definition; yet some endeavour must be made to indicate the direction in which we must feel for this great truth if we are to find it. The idea is that of realizing personality without that selfhood which differentiates one individual from another. "I am not that other because I am myself"— this is the definition of individual selfhood; but it necessarily imparts the idea of limitation, because the recognition of any other individuality at once affirms a point at which our own individuality ceases and the other begins. Now this mode of recognition cannot be attributed to the Universal Mind. For it to recognize a point where itself ceased and something else began would be to recognize itself as *not* universal; for the meaning of universality is the including of *all* things, and therefore for this intelligence to recognize anything as being *outside itself* would be a denial of its own being. We may therefore say without hesitation that, whatever may be the nature of its intelligence, it must be entirely devoid of the element of self-recognition *as an individual personality* on any scale whatever. Seen in this light it is at once clear that the originating all-pervading Spirit is the grand impersonal principle of Life which gives rise to all the particular manifestations of Nature. Its absolute impersonalness, in the sense of the entire absence of any consciousness of *individual* selfhood, is a point on which it is impossible to insist too strongly. The attributing of an impossible individuality to the Universal Mind is one of the two grand errors which we find sapping the foundations of religion and philosophy in all ages. The other consists in rushing to the opposite extreme and denying the quality of personal intelligence to the Universal Mind. The answer to this error remains, as of old, in the simple question, "He that made the eye shall He not see? He that planted the ear shall He not hear?"—or to use a popular proverb, "You cannot get out of a bag more than there is in it"; and consequently the fact that we ourselves are centres of personal intelligence is proof that the infinite, from which these centres are concentrated, must be infinite intelligence, and thus we cannot avoid attributing to it the two factors which constitute personality, namely, intelligence and volition. We are therefore brought to the conclusion that this universally diffused essence, which we might think of as a sort of spiritual protoplasm, must possess all the qualities of personality without that conscious recognition of self which constitutes separate individuality; and since the word "personality" has become so associated in our ordinary talk with the idea of "individuality" it will perhaps be better to coin a new word, and speak of the personalness of the Universal Mind as indicating its personal *quality*, apart from individuality. We must realize that this universal spirit permeates all space and all manifested substance, just as physical scientists tell us that the ether does, and that wherever it is, there it must carry with it all that it is in its own being; and we shall then see that we are in the midst of an ocean of undifferentiated yet intelligent Life, above, below, and all around, and permeating ourselves both mentally and corporeally, and all other beings as well.

Gradually as we come to realize the truth of this statement, our eyes will begin to open to its immense significance. It means that all Nature is pervaded by an interior personalness, infinite in its potentialities of intelligence, responsiveness, and power of expression, and only waiting to be called into activity by our recognition of it. By the terms of its nature it can respond to us only as we recognize it. If we are at that intellectual level where we can see nothing but chance governing the world, then this underlying universal mind will present to us nothing but a fortuitous confluence of forces without any intelligible order. If we are sufficiently advanced to see that such a confluence could only produce a chaos, and not a cosmos, then our conceptions expand to the idea of universal Law, and we find *this* to be the nature of the all-underlying principle. We have made an immense advance from the realm of mere accident into a world where there are definite principles on which we can calculate with certainty *when we know them*. But here is the crucial point. The laws of the universe are there, but we are ignorant of them, and only through experience gained by repeated failures can we get any insight into the laws with which we have to deal. How painful each step and how slow the progress! Æons upon æons would not suffice to grasp all the laws of the universe in their totality, not in the visible world only, but also in the world of the unseen; each failure to know the true law implies suffering arising from our ignorant breach of it; and thus, since Nature is infinite, we are met by the paradox that we must in some way contrive to compass the knowledge of the infinite with our individual intelligence, and we must perform a pilgrimage along an unceasing Via Dolorosa beneath the lash of the inexorable Law until we find the solution to the problem. But it will be asked, May we not go on until at last we attain the possession of all knowledge? People do not realize what is meant by "the infinite," or they would not ask such questions. The infinite is that which is limitless and exhaustless. Imagine the vastest capacity you will, and having filled it with the infinite, what remains of the infinite is just as infinite as before. To the mathematician this may be put very clearly. Raise x to any power you will, and however vast may be the disparity between it and the lower powers of x, both are equally incommensurate with x^n. The universal reign of Law is a magnificent truth; it is one of the two great pillars of the universe symbolized by the two pillars that stood at the entrance to Solomon's temple: it is Jachin, but Jachin must be equilibriated by Boaz.

It is an enduring truth, which can never be altered, that every infraction of the Law of Nature must carry its punitive consequences with it. We can never get beyond the range of cause and effect. There is no escaping from the law of punishment, except by knowledge. If we know a law of Nature and work with it, we shall find it our unfailing friend, ever ready to serve us, and never rebuking us for past failures; but if we ignorantly or wilfully transgress it, it is our implacable enemy, until we again become obedient to it; and therefore the only redemption from perpetual pain and servitude is by a self-expansion which can grasp infinitude itself. How is this to be accomplished? By our progress to that kind and degree of intelligence by which we realize the inherent *personalness* of the divine all-pervading Life, which is at once the Law and the Substance of all that is. Well said the Jewish rabbis of old, "The Law is a Person." When we once realize that the universal Life and the universal Law are one with the universal Personalness, then we have established the pillar Boaz as the needed complement to Jachin; and when we find the common point in which these two unite, we have raised the Royal Arch through which we may triumphantly enter the Temple. We must dissociate the Universal Personalness from every conception of individuality. The universal can never be the individual; that would be a contradiction in terms. But because the universal personalness is the root of all individual personalities, it finds its highest expression in response to those who realize its personal nature. And it is this recognition that solves the seemingly insoluble paradox. The only way to attain that knowledge of the Infinite Law which will change the Via Dolorosa into the Path of Joy is to embody in ourselves a *principle* of knowledge commensurate with the infinitude of that which is to be known; and this is accomplished by realizing that, infinite as the law itself, is a universal Intelligence in the midst of which we float as in a living ocean. Intelligence without individual personality, but which, in producing us, concentrates itself into the personal individualities which we are. What should be the relation of such an intelligence towards us? Not one of favouritism; not any more than the Law can it respect one person above another, for itself is the root and support for each alike. Not one of refusal to our advances; for without individuality it can have no personal object of its own to conflict with ours; and since it is itself the origin of all individual intelligence, it cannot be shut off by inability to understand. By the very terms of its being, therefore, this infinite, underlying, all-producing Mind must be ready immediately to respond to all who realize their true relation to it. As the very principle of Life itself it must be infinitely susceptible to feeling, and consequently it will reproduce with absolute accuracy whatever conception of itself we impress upon it; and hence if we realize the human mind as that stage in the evolution of the cosmic order at which an individuality has arisen capable of expressing, not merely the livingness, but also the personalness of the universal underlying spirit, then we see that its most perfect mode of self-expression must be by identifying itself with these individual personalities.

The identification is, of course, limited by the measure of the individual intelligence, meaning, not merely the intellectual perception of the sequence of cause and effect, but also that indescribable reciprocity of *feeling* by which we instinctively recognize something in another making them akin to ourselves; and so it is that when we intelligently realize that the innermost principle of being must, by reason of its universality, have a common nature with our own, then we have solved the paradox of universal knowledge, for we have realized our identity of being with the Universal Mind, which is commensurate with the Universal Law. Thus we arrive at the truth of St. John's statement, "Ye know all things," only this knowledge is primarily on the spiritual plane. It is not brought out into intellectual statement whether needed or not; for it is not in itself the specific knowledge of particular facts, but it is the undifferentiated principle of knowledge which we may differentiate in any direction that we choose. This is a philosophical necessity of the case, for though the action of the individual mind consists in differentiating the universal into particular applications, to differentiate the *whole* universal would be a contradiction in terms; and so, because we cannot exhaust the infinite, our possession of it must consist in our power to differentiate it as the occasion may require, the only limit being that which we ourselves assign to the manifestation.

In this way, then, the recognition of the community of *personality* between ourselves and the universal undifferentiated Spirit, which is the root and substance of all things, solves the question of our release from the iron grasp of an inflexible Law, not by abrogating the Law, which would mean the annihilation of all things, but by producing in us an intelligence equal in affinity with the universal Law itself, and thus enabling us to apprehend and meet the requirements of the Law in each particular as it arises. In this way the Cosmic Intelligence becomes individualized, and the individual intelligence becomes universalized; the two become one, and in proportion as this unity is realized and acted on, it will be found that the Law, which gives rise to all outward conditions, whether of body or of circumstances, becomes more and more clearly understood, and can therefore be more freely made use of, so that by steady, intelligent endeavour to unfold upon these lines we may reach degrees of power to which it is impossible to assign any limits. The student who would understand the rationale of the unfoldment of his own possibilities must make no mistake here. He must realize that the whole process is that of bringing the universal within the grasp of the individual by raising the individual to the level of the universal and not vice-versa. It is a mathematical truism that you cannot contract the infinite, and that you *can* expand the individual; and it is precisely on these lines that evolution works. The laws of nature cannot be altered in the least degree; but we can come into such a realization of our own relation to the universal principle of Law that underlies them as to be able to press all particular laws, whether of the visible or invisible side of Nature, into our service and so find ourselves masters of the situation. This is to be accomplished by knowledge; and the only knowledge which will effect this purpose in all its measureless immensity is the knowledge of the personal element in Universal Spirit in its reciprocity to our own personality. Our recognition of this Spirit must therefore be twofold, as the principle of necessary sequence, order or Law, and also as the principle of Intelligence, responsive to our own recognition of it.

8

RECIPROCAL ACTION OF THE UNIVERSAL AND INDIVIDUAL MINDS

It must be admitted that the foregoing considerations bring us to the borders of theological speculation, but the student must bear in mind that as a Mental Scientist it is his business to regard even the most exalted spiritual phenomena from a purely scientific standpoint, which is that of the working of a universal natural Law. If he thus simply deals with the facts as he finds them, there is little doubt that the true meaning of many theological statements will become clear to him; but he will do well to lay it down as a general rule that it is not necessary either to the use or understanding of any law, whether on the personal or the impersonal side of Nature, that we should give a theological explanation of it. Although, therefore, the personal quality inherent in the universal underlying spirit, which is present in all things, cannot be too strongly insisted upon, we must remember that in dealing with it we are still dealing with a purely natural power which reappears at every point with protean variety of form, whether as person, animal, or thing. In each case what it becomes to any individual is exactly measured by that individual's recognition of it. To each and all it bears the relation of supporter of the race, and where the individual development is incapable of realizing anything more, this is the limit of the relation; but as the individual's power of recognition expands, he finds a reciprocal expansion on the part of this intelligent power which gradually develops into the consciousness of intimate companionship between the individualized mind and the unindividualized source of it.

Now this is exactly the relation which, on ordinary scientific principles, we should expect to find between the individual and the cosmic mind, on the supposition that the cosmic mind is subjective mind, and for reasons already given we can regard it in no other light. As subjective mind it must reproduce exactly the conception of itself which the objective mind of the individual, acting through his own subjective mind, impresses upon it; and at the same time, as creative mind, it builds up external facts in correspondence with this conception. *Quot homines tot sententiæ*: each one externalizes in his outward circumstances precisely his idea of the Universal Mind; and the man who realizes that by the natural law of mind he can bring the Universal Mind into perfectly reciprocal action with his own, will on the one hand make it a source of infinite instruction, and on the other a source of infinite power. He will thus wisely alternate the personal and impersonal aspects respectively between his individual mind and the Universal Mind; when he is seeking for guidance or strength he will regard his own mind as the impersonal element which is to *receive personality* from the superior wisdom and force of the Greater Mind; and when, on the other hand, he is to give out the stores thus accumulated, he must reverse the position and consider his own mind as the personal element, and the Universal Mind as the impersonal, which he can therefore *direct* with certainty by impressing his own personal desire upon it. We need not be staggered at the greatness of this conclusion, for it follows necessarily from the natural relation between the subjective and the objective minds; and the only question is whether we will limit our view to the lower level of the latter, or expand it so as to take in the limitless possibilities which the subjective mind presents to us.

I have dealt with this question at some length because it affords the key to two very important subjects: the Law of Supply and the nature of Intuition. Students often find it easier to understand how the mind can influence the body with which it is so intimately associated, than how it can influence circumstances. If the operation of thought-power were confined exclusively to the individual mind this difficulty might arise; but if there is one lesson the student of Mental Science should take to heart more than another, it is that the action of thought-power is not limited to a circumscribed individuality. What the individual does is to *give direction* to something which is unlimited, to call into action a force infinitely greater than his own, which because it is in itself impersonal though intelligent, will receive the impress of his personality, and can therefore make its influence felt far beyond the limits which bound the individual's objective perception of the circumstances with which he has to deal. It is for this reason that I lay so much stress on the combination of two apparent opposites in the Universal Mind, the union of intelligence with impersonality. The intelligence not only enables it to receive the impress of our thought, but also causes it to devise exactly the right *means* for bringing it into accomplishment. This is only the logical result of the hypothesis that we are dealing with infinite Intelligence which is also infinite Life. Life means Power, and infinite life therefore means limitless power; and limitless power moved by limitless intelligence cannot be conceived of as ever stopping short of the accomplishment of its object; therefore, given the *intention* on the part of the Universal Mind, there can be no doubt as to its ultimate accomplishment. Then comes the question of intention. How do we know what the intention of the Universal Mind may be? Here comes in the element of impersonality. It has *no intention*, because it is *impersonal*. As I have already said, the Universal mind works by a law of averages for the advancement of the race, and is in no way concerned with the particular wishes of the individual. If his wishes are in line with the forward movement of the everlasting principle, there is nowhere in Nature any power to restrict him in their fulfilment. If they are opposed to the general forward movement, then they will bring him into collision with it, and it will crush him. From the relation between them it results that the same principle which shows itself in the individual mind as Will, becomes in the universal mind a Law of Tendency; and the direction of this tendency must always be to life-givingness, because the universal mind is the undifferentiated Life-spirit of the universe. Therefore in every case the test is whether our particular intention is in this same lifeward direction; and if it is, then we may be absolutely certain that there is no intention on the part of the Universal Mind to thwart the intention of our own individual mind; we are dealing with a purely impersonal force, and it will no more oppose us by specific plans of its own than will steam or electricity. Combining then, these two aspects of the Universal Mind, its utter impersonality and its perfect intelligence, we find precisely the sort of natural force we are in want of, something which will undertake whatever we put into its hands without asking questions or bargaining for terms, and which, having undertaken our business, will bring to bear on it an intelligence to which the united knowledge of the whole human race is as nothing, and a power equal to this intelligence. I may be using a rough and ready mode of expression, but my object is to bring home to the student the nature of the power he can employ and the method of employing it, and I may therefore state the whole position thus: Your object is not to run the whole cosmos, but to draw particular benefits, physical, mental, moral, or financial into your own or someone else's life. From this individual point of view the universal creative power has no mind of its own, and therefore you can make up its mind for it. When its mind is thus made up for it, it never abrogates its place as the creative power, but at once sets to work to carry out the purpose for which it has thus been concentrated; and unless this concentration is dissipated by the same agency (yourself) which first produced it, it will work on by the law of growth to complete manifestation on the outward plane.

In dealing with this great impersonal intelligence, we are dealing with the infinite, and we must fully realize infinitude as that which touches all points, and if it does, there should be no difficulty in understanding that this intelligence can draw together the means requisite for its purpose even from the ends of the world; and therefore, realizing the Law according to which the result can be produced, we must resolutely put aside all questioning as to the specific means which will be employed in any case. To question this is to sow that very seed of doubt which it is our first object to eradicate, and our intellectual endeavour should therefore be directed, not to the attempt to foretell the various secondary causes which will eventually combine to produce the desired result, laying down beforehand what particular causes should be necessary, and from what quarter they should come; but we should direct our intellectual endeavour to seeing more clearly the rationale of the general law by which trains of secondary causes are set in motion. Employed in the former way our intellect becomes the greatest hindrance to our success, for it only helps to increase our doubts, since it is trying to grasp particulars which at the time are entirely outside its circle of vision; but employed in the latter it affords the most material aid in maintaining that nucleus without which there is no centre from which the principle of growth can assert itself. The intellect can only deduce consequences from facts which it is able to state, and consequently cannot deduce any assurance from facts of whose existence it cannot yet have any knowledge through the medium of the outward senses; but for the same reason it can realize the existence of a *Law* by which the as yet unmanifested circumstances may be brought into manifestation. Thus used in its right order, the intellect becomes the handmaid of that more interior power within us which manipulates the unseen substance of all things, and which we may call relative first cause.

9

CAUSES AND CONDITIONS

THE EXPRESSION "*relative* first cause" has been used in the last section to distinguish the action of the creative principle in the *individual* mind from Universal First Cause on the one hand and from secondary causes on the other. As it exists in *us*, primary causation is the power to initiate a train of causation directed to an individual purpose. As the power of initiating a fresh sequence of cause and effect it is first cause, and as referring to an individual purpose it is relative, and it may therefore be spoken of as relative first cause, or the power of primary causation manifested by the individual. The understanding and use of this power is the whole object of Mental Science, and it is therefore necessary that the student should clearly see the relation between causes and conditions. A simple illustration will go further for this purpose than any elaborate explanation. If a lighted candle is brought into a room the room becomes illuminated, and if the candle is taken away it becomes dark again. Now the illumination and the darkness are both conditions, the one positive resulting from the presence of the light, and the other negative resulting from its absence. From this simple example we therefore see that every positive condition has an exactly opposite negative condition corresponding to it, and that this correspondence results from their being related to the *same cause*, the one positively and the other negatively; and hence we may lay down the rule that all positive conditions result from the active presence of a certain cause, and all negative conditions from the absence of such a cause. A condition, whether positive or negative, is never *primary* cause, and the *primary* cause of any series can never be negative, for negation is the condition which arises from the absence of active causation. This should be thoroughly understood as it is the philosophic basis of all those "denials" which play so important a part in Mental Science, and which may be summed up in the statement that evil being negative, or privation of good, has no substantive existence in itself. Conditions, however, whether positive or negative, are no sooner called into existence than they become causes in their turn and produce further conditions, and so on *ad infinitum*, thus giving rise to the whole train of secondary causes. So long as we judge only from the information conveyed to us by the outward senses, we are working on the plane of secondary causation and see nothing but a succession of conditions, forming part of an endless train of antecedent conditions coming out of the past and stretching away into the future, and from this point of view we are under the rule of an iron destiny from which there seems no possibility of escape. This is because the outward senses are only capable of dealing with the relations which one mode of limitation bears to another, for they are the instruments by which we take cognizance of the relative and the conditioned. Now the only way of escape is by rising out of the region of secondary causes into that of primary causation, where the originating energy is to be found before it has yet passed into manifestation as a condition. This region is to be found *within ourselves*; it is the region of pure ideas; and it is for this reason that I have laid stress on the two aspects of spirit as pure thought and manifested form. The thought-image or ideal pattern of a thing is the *first cause* relatively to that thing; it is the substance of that thing untrammelled by any antecedent conditions.

If we realize that all visible things *must* have their origin in spirit, then the whole creation around us is the standing evidence that the starting-point of all things is in thought-images or ideas, for no other action than the formation of such images can be conceived of spirit prior to its manifestation in matter. If, then, this is spirit's modus operandi for self-expression, we have only to transfer this conception from the scale of cosmic spirit working on the plane of the universal to that of individualized spirit working on the plane of the particular, to see that the formation of an ideal image by means of our thought is setting first cause in motion with regard to this specific object. There is no difference in kind between the operation of first cause in the universal and in the particular; the difference is only a difference of scale, but the power itself is identical. We must therefore always be very clear as to whether we are *consciously* using first cause or not. Note the word "consciously" because, whether consciously or unconsciously, we are always using first cause; and it was for this reason I emphasized the fact that the Universal Mind is purely subjective and therefore bound by the laws which apply to subjective mind on whatever scale. Hence we are *always* impressing some sort of ideas upon it, whether we are aware of the fact or not, and all our existing limitations result from our having habitually impressed upon it that idea of limitation which we have imbibed by restricting all possibility to the region of secondary causes. But now when investigation has shown us that conditions are never causes in *themselves*, but only the subsequent links of a chain started on the plane of the pure ideal, what we have to do is to reverse our method of thinking and regard the ideal as the real, and the outward manifestation as a mere reflection which must change with every change of the object which casts it. For these reasons it is essential to know whether we are consciously making use of first cause with a definite purpose or not, and the criterion is this. If we regard the fulfilment of our purpose as contingent upon any *circumstances*, past, present, or future, we are not making use of first cause; we have descended to the level of secondary causation, which is the region of doubts, fears, and limitations, all of which we are impressing upon the universal subjective mind with the inevitable result that it will build up corresponding external conditions. But if we realize that the region of secondary causes is the region of mere reflections we shall not think of our purpose as contingent on any conditions whatever, but shall know that by forming the idea of it in the absolute, and maintaining that idea, we have shaped the first cause into the desired form and can await the result with cheerful expectancy.

It is here that we find the importance of realizing spirit's independence of time and space. An ideal, as such, cannot be formed in the future. It must either be formed here and now or not be formed at all; and it is for this reason that every teacher who has ever spoken with due knowledge of the subject has impressed upon his followers the necessity of picturing to themselves the fulfilment of their desires as *already accomplished* on the spiritual plane, as the indispensable condition of fulfilment in the visible and concrete.

When this is properly understood, any anxious thought as to the *means* to be employed in the accomplishment of our purposes is seen to be quite unnecessary. If the end is already secured, then it follows that all the steps leading to it are secured also. The means will pass into the smaller circle of our conscious activities day by day in due order, and then we have to work upon them, not with fear, doubt, or feverish excitement, but calmly and joyously, because we *know* that the end is already secured, and that our reasonable use of such means as present themselves in the desired direction is only one portion of a much larger coordinated movement, the final result of which admits of no doubt. Mental Science does not offer a premium to idleness, but it takes all work out of the region of anxiety and toil by assuring the worker of the success of his labour, if not in the precise form he anticipated, then in some other still better suited to his requirements. But suppose, when we reach a point where some momentous decision has to be made, we happen to decide wrongly? On the hypothesis that the end is already secured you cannot decide wrongly. Your right decision is as much one of the necessary steps in the accomplishment of the end as any of the other conditions leading up to it, and therefore, while being careful to avoid rash action, we may make sure that the same Law which is controlling the rest of the circumstances in the right direction will influence our judgment in that direction also. To get good results we must properly understand our relation to the great impersonal power we are using. It is intelligent and we are intelligent, and the two intelligences must cooperate. We must not fly in the face of the Law by expecting it to do *for* us what it can only do *through* us; and we must therefore use our intelligence with the knowledge that it is acting *as the instrument of a greater intelligence*; and because we have this knowledge we may, and should, cease from all anxiety as to the final result. In actual practice we must first form the ideal conception of our object with the definite intention of impressing it upon the universal mind—it is this intention which takes such thought out of the region of mere casual fancies—and then affirm that our knowledge of the Law is sufficient reason for a calm expectation of a corresponding result, and that therefore all necessary conditions will come to us in due order. We can then turn to the affairs of our daily life with the calm assurance that the initial conditions are either there already or will soon come into view. If we do not at once see them, let us rest content with the knowledge that the spiritual prototype is already in existence and wait till some circumstance pointing in the desired direction begins to show itself. It may be a very small circumstance, but it is the direction and not the magnitude which is to be taken into consideration. As soon as we see it we should regard it as the first sprouting of the seed we have sown in the Absolute, and do calmly, and without excitement, whatever the circumstances may seem to require, and then later on we shall see that this doing will in turn lead to further circumstances in the same direction until we find ourselves conducted step by step to the accomplishment of our object. In this way the understanding of the great principle of the Law of Supply will, by repeated experiences, deliver us more and more completely out of the region of anxious thought and toilsome labour and bring us into a new world where the useful employment of all our powers, whether mental or physical, will only be an unfolding of our individuality upon the lines of its own nature, and therefore a perpetual source of health and happiness; a sufficient inducement, surely, to the careful study of the laws governing the relation between the individual and the Universal Mind.

10

INTUITION

WE HAVE SEEN that the subjective mind is amenable to suggestion by the objective mind; but there is also an action of the subjective mind upon the objective. The individual's subjective mind is his own innermost self, and its first care is the maintenance of the individuality of which it is the foundation; and since it is pure spirit it has its continual existence in that plane of being where all things subsist in the universal here and the everlasting now, and consequently can inform the lower mind of things removed from its ken either by distance or futurity. As the absence of the conditions of time and space must logically concentrate all things into a present focus, we can assign no limit to the subjective mind's power of perception, and therefore the question arises, why does it not keep the objective mind continually informed on all points? And the answer is that it would do so if the objective mind were sufficiently trained to recognize the indications given, and to effect this training is one of the purposes of Mental Science. When once we recognize the position of the subjective mind as the supporter of the whole individuality we cannot doubt that much of what we take to be the spontaneous movement of the objective mind has its origin in the subjective mind prompting the objective mind in the right direction without our being consciously aware of it. But at times when the urgency of the case seems to demand it, or when, for some reason yet unknown, the objective mind is for a while more closely *en rapport* with the subjective mind, the interior voice is heard strongly and persistently; and when this is the case we do well to pay heed to it. Want of space forbids me to give examples, but doubtless such will not be wanting in the reader's experience.

The importance of understanding and following the intuition cannot be exaggerated, but I candidly admit the great practical difficulty of keeping the happy mean between the disregard of the interior voice and allowing ourselves to be run away with by groundless fancies. The best guide is the knowledge that comes of personal experience which gradually leads to the acquisition of a sort of inward sense of touch that enables us to distinguish the true from the false, and which appears to grow with the sincere desire for truth and with the recognition of the spirit as its source. The only general principles the writer can deduce from his own experience are that when, in spite of all appearances pointing in the direction of a certain line of conduct, there is still a persistent *feeling* that it should not be followed, in the majority of instances it will be found that the argument of the objective mind, however correct on the facts objectively known, was deficient from ignorance of facts which could not be objectively known at the time, but which were known to the intuitive faculty. Another principle is that our *very first* impression or feeling on any subject is generally correct. Before the objective mind has begun to argue on the subject it is like the surface of a smooth lake which clearly reflects the light from above; but as soon as it begins to argue from outside appearances these also throw their reflections upon its surface, so that the original image becomes blurred and is no longer recognizable. This first conception is very speedily lost, and it should therefore be carefully observed and registered in the memory with a view to testing the various arguments which will subsequently arise on the objective plane. It is, however, impossible to reduce so interior an action as that of the intuition to the form of hard and fast rules, and beyond carefully noting particular cases as they occur, probably the best plan for the student will be to include the whole subject of intuition in the general principle of the Law of Attraction, especially if he sees how this law interacts with that personal quality of universal spirit of which we have already spoken.

11

HEALING

THE SUBJECT of healing has been elaborately treated by many writers and fully deserves all the attention that has been given to it, but the object of these lectures is rather to ground the student in those general principles on which *all* conscious use of the creative power of thought is based, than to lay down formal rules for specific applications of it. I will therefore examine the broad principles which appear to be common to the various methods of mental healing which are in use, each of which derives its efficacy, not from the peculiarity of the method, but from it being such a method as allows the higher laws of Nature to come into play. Now the principle universally laid down by all mental healers, in whatever various terms they may explain it, is that the basis of all healing is a change in belief. The sequence from which this results is as follows: the subjective mind is the creative faculty within us, and creates whatever the objective mind impresses upon it; the objective mind, or intellect, impresses its thought upon it; the thought is the expression of the belief; hence whatever the subjective mind creates is the reproduction externally of our beliefs. Accordingly our whole object is to change our beliefs, and we cannot do this without some solid ground of conviction of the falsity of our old beliefs and of the truth of our new ones, and this ground we find in that law of causation which I have endeavoured to explain. The wrong belief, which externalizes as sickness, is the belief that some secondary cause, which is really only a condition, is a primary cause. The knowledge of the law shows that there is only *one* primary cause, and this is the factor which in our own individuality we call subjective or subconscious mind. For this reason I have insisted on the difference between placing an idea in the subconscious mind, that is, on the plane of the absolute and without reference to time and space, and placing the same idea in the conscious intellectual mind, which only perceives things as related to time and space. Now the only conception you can have of *yourself* in the absolute, or unconditioned, is as *purely living Spirit*, not hampered by conditions of any sort, and therefore not subject to illness; and when this idea is firmly impressed on the subconscious mind, it will externalize it. The reason why this process is not always successful at the first attempt is that all our life we have been holding the false belief in sickness as a substantial entity in itself and thus being a primary cause, instead of being merely a negative *condition* resulting from the *absence* of a primary cause; and a belief which has become ingrained from childhood cannot be eradicated at a moment's notice. We often find, therefore, that for some time after a treatment there is an improvement in the patient's health, and then the old symptoms return. This is because the new belief in his own creative faculty has not yet had time to penetrate down to the innermost depths of the subconscious mind, but has only partially entered it. Each succeeding treatment strengthens the subconscious mind in its hold of the new belief until at last a permanent cure is effected. This is the method of self-treatment based on the patient's own knowledge of the law of his being.

But "there is not in all men this knowledge," or at any rate not such a full recognition of it as will enable them to give successful treatment to themselves, and in these cases the intervention of the healer becomes necessary. The only difference between the healer and the patient is that the healer has learnt how to control the less self-conscious modes of the spirit by the more self-conscious mode, while the patient has not yet attained to this knowledge; and what the healer does is to substitute his own objective or conscious mentality, which is will joined to intellect, for that of the patient, and in this way to find entrance to his subconscious mind and impress upon it the suggestion of perfect health.

The question then arises, how can the healer substitute his own conscious mind for that of the patient? and the answer shows the practical application of those very abstract principles which I have laid down in the earlier sections. Our ordinary conception of ourselves is that of an individual personality which ends where another personality begins, in other words that the two personalities are entirely separate. This is an error. There is no such hard and fast line of demarcation between personalities, and the boundaries between one and another can be increased or reduced in rigidity according to will, in fact they may be temporarily removed so completely that, for the time being, the two personalities become merged into one. Now the action which takes place between healer and patient depends on this principle. The patient is asked by the healer to put himself in a receptive mental attitude, which means that he is to exercise his volition for the purpose of removing the barrier of his own objective personality and thus affording entrance to the mental power of the healer. On his side also the healer does the same thing, only with this difference, that while the patient withdraws the barrier on his side with the intention of admitting a flowing-in, the healer does so with the intention of allowing a flowing-out, and thus by the joint action of the two minds the barriers of both personalities are removed and the direction of the flow of volition is determined; that is to say, it flows from the healer as actively willing to give, towards the patient as passively willing to receive, according to the universal law of Nature that the flow must always be from the *plenum* to the *vacuum*. This mutual removal of the external mental barrier between healer and patient is what is termed establishing a *rapport* between them, and here we find one most valuable practical application of the principle laid down earlier in this book, that pure spirit is present in its entirety at every point simultaneously. It is for this reason that as soon as the healer realizes that the barriers of external personality between himself and his patient have been removed, he can then speak to the subconscious mind of the patient as though it were his own, for both being pure spirit the *thought* of their identity *makes* them identical, and both are concentrated into a single entity at a single point upon which the conscious mind of the healer can be brought to bear, according to the universal principle of the control of the subjective mind by the objective mind through suggestion. It is for this reason I have insisted on the distinction between *pure* spirit, or spirit conceived of apart from extension in any matrix, and the conception of it as so extended. If we concentrate our mind upon the diseased condition of the patient we are thinking of him as a separate personality, and are not fixing our mind upon that conception of him as pure spirit which will afford us effectual entry to his springs of being. We must therefore withdraw our thought from the contemplation of symptoms, and indeed from his corporeal personality altogether, and must think of him as a purely spiritual individuality, and as such entirely free from subjection to any conditions, and consequently as voluntarily externalizing the conditions most expressive of the vitality and intelligence which pure spirit is. Thinking of him thus, we then make mental affirmation that he shall build up outwardly the correspondence of that perfect vitality which he knows himself to be inwardly; and this suggestion being impressed by the healer's conscious thought, while the patient's conscious thought is at the same time impressing the fact that he is receiving the active thought of the healer, the result is that the patient's subconscious mind becomes thoroughly imbued with the recognition of its own life-giving power, and according to the recognized law of subjective mentality proceeds to work out this suggestion into external manifestation, and thus health is substituted for sickness.

It must be understood that the purpose of the process here described is to strengthen the subject's individuality, not to dominate it. To use it for domination is *inversion*, bringing its appropriate penalty to the operator.

In this description I have contemplated the case where the patient is consciously cooperating with the healer, and it is in order to obtain this cooperation that the mental healer usually makes a point of instructing the patient in the broad principles of Mental Science, if he is not already acquainted with them. But this is not always advisable or possible. Sometimes the statement of principles opposed to existing prejudices arouses opposition, and any active antagonism on the patient's part must tend to intensify the barrier of conscious personality which it is the healer's first object to remove. In these cases nothing is so effective as *absent treatment*. If the student has grasped all that has been said on the subject of spirit and matter, he will see that in mental treatment time and space count for nothing, because the whole action takes place on a plane where these conditions do not obtain; and it is therefore quite immaterial whether the patient be in the immediate presence of the healer or in a distant country. Under these circumstances it is found by experience that one of the most effectual modes of mental healing is by treatment during sleep, because then the patient's whole system is naturally in a state of relaxation which prevents him offering any conscious opposition to the treatment. And by the same rule the healer also is able to treat even more effectively during his own sleep than while waking. Before going to sleep he firmly impresses on his subjective mind that it is to convey curative suggestion to the subjective mind of the patient, and then, by the general principles of the relation between subjective and objective mind this suggestion is carried out during all the hours that the conscious individuality is wrapped in repose. This method is applicable to young children to whom the principles of the science cannot be explained; and also to persons at a distance: and indeed the only advantage gained by the personal meeting of the patient and healer is in the instruction that can be orally given, or when the patient is at that early stage of knowledge where the healer's visible presence conveys the suggestion that something is then being done which could not be done in his absence; otherwise the presence or absence of the patient are matters perfectly indifferent. The student must always recollect that the subconscious mind does not have to work *through* the intellect or conscious mind to produce its curative effects. It is part of the all-pervading creative force of Nature, while the intellect is not creative but distributive.

From mental healing it is but a step to telepathy, clairvoyance and other kindred manifestations of transcendental power which are from time to time exhibited by the subjective entity and which follow laws as accurate as those which govern what we are accustomed to consider our more normal faculties; but these subjects do not properly fall within the scope of a book whose purpose is to lay down the broad principles which underlie *all* spiritual phenomena. Until these are clearly understood the student cannot profitably attempt the detailed study of the more interior powers; for to do so without a firm foundation of knowledge and some experience in its practical application would only be to expose himself to unknown dangers, and would be contrary to the scientific principle that the advance into the unknown can only be made from the standpoint of the known, otherwise we only come into a confused region of guess-work without any clearly defined principles for our guidance.

12

THE WILL

THE WILL IS of such primary importance that the student should be on his guard against any mistake as to the position which it holds in the mental economy. Many writers and teachers insist on will-power as though that were the creative faculty. No doubt intense will-power can evolve certain external results, but like all other methods of compulsion it lacks the permanency of natural growth. The appearances, forms, and conditions produced by mere intensity of will-power will only hang together so long as the compelling force continues; but let it be exhausted or withdrawn, and the elements thus forced into unnatural combination will at once fly back to their proper affinities; the form created by compulsion never had the germ of vitality *in itself* and is therefore dissipated as soon as the external energy which supported it is withdrawn. The mistake is in attributing the creative power to the will, or perhaps I should say in attributing the creative power to ourselves at all. The truth is that man never creates anything. His function is, not to create, but to combine and distribute that which is already in being, and what we call our creations are new combinations of already existing material, whether mental or corporeal. This is amply demonstrated in the physical sciences. No one speaks of creating energy, but only of transforming one form of energy into another; and if we realize this as a universal principle, we shall see that on the mental plane as well as on the physical we never create energy but only provide the conditions by which the energy already existing in one mode can exhibit itself in another; therefore what, relatively to man, we call his creative power, is that receptive attitude of expectancy which, so to say, makes a mould into which the plastic and as yet undifferentiated substance can flow and take the desired form. The will has much the same place in our mental machinery that the toolholder has in a power-lathe: it is not the power, but it keeps the mental faculties in that position relatively to the power which enables it to do the desired work. If, using the word in its widest sense, we may say that the imagination is the creative function, we may call the will the centralizing principle. Its function is to keep the imagination centred in the right direction. We are aiming at consciously controlling our mental powers instead of letting them hurry us hither and thither in a purposeless manner, and we must therefore understand the relation of these powers to each other for the production of external results. First the whole train of causation is started by some emotion which gives rise to a desire; next the judgment determines whether we shall externalize this desire or not; then the desire having been approved by the judgment, the will comes forward and directs the imagination to form the necessary spiritual prototype; and the imagination thus centered on a particular object creates the spiritual nucleus, which in its turn acts as a centre round which the forces of attraction begin to work, and continue to operate until, by the law of growth, the concrete result becomes perceptible to our external senses.

The business of the will, then, is to retain the various faculties of our mind in that position where they are really doing the work we wish, and this position may be generalized into the three following attitudes: either we wish to act upon something, or be acted on by it, or to maintain a neutral position; in other words we either intend to project a force, or receive a force, or keep a position of inactivity relatively to some particular object. Now the judgment determines which of these three positions we shall take up, the consciously active, the consciously receptive, or the consciously neutral; and then the function of the will is simply to maintain the position we have determined upon; and if we maintain any given mental attitude we may reckon with all certainty on the law of attraction drawing us to those correspondences which exteriorly symbolize the attitude in question. This is very different from the semi-animal screwing-up of the nervous forces which, with some people, stands for will-power. It implies no strain on the nervous system and is consequently not followed by any sense of exhaustion. The will-power, when transferred from the region of the lower mentality to the spiritual plane, becomes simply a calm and peaceful determination to retain a certain mental attitude in spite of all temptations to the contrary, knowing that by doing so the desired result will certainly appear.

The training of the will and its transference from the lower to the higher plane of our nature are among the first objects of Mental Science. The man is summed up in his will. Whatever he does by his own will is his own act; whatever he does without the consent of his will is not his own act but that of the power by which his will was coerced; but we must recognize that, on the mental plane, no other individuality can obtain control over our will unless we first allow it to do so; and it is for this reason that all legitimate use of Mental Science is towards the strengthening of the will, whether in ourselves or others, and bringing it under the control of an enlightened reason. When the will realizes its power to deal with first cause it is no longer necessary for the operator to state to himself *in extenso* all the philosophy of its action every time he wishes to use it, but, knowing that the trained will is a tremendous spiritual force acting on the plane of first cause, he simply expresses his desire with the intention of operating on that plane, and knows that the desire thus expressed will in due time externalize itself as concrete fact. He now sees that the point which really demands his earnest attention is not whether he possesses the power of externalizing any results he chooses, but of learning to choose wisely what results to produce. For let us not suppose that even the highest powers will take us out of the law of cause and effect. We can never set any cause in motion without calling forth those effects which it already contains in embryo and which will again become causes in their turn, thus producing a series which must continue to flow on until it is cut short by bringing into operation a cause of an opposite character to the one which originated it. Thus we shall find the field for the exercise of our intelligence continually expanding with the expansion of our powers; for, granted a good intention, we shall always wish to contemplate the results of our action as far as our intelligence will permit. We may not be able to see very far, but there is one safe general principle to be gained from what has already been said about causes and conditions, which is that the whole sequence always partakes of the same character as the initial cause; if that character is negative, that is, destitute of any desire to externalize kindness, cheerfulness, strength, beauty or some other sort of good, this negative quality will make itself felt all down the line; but if the opposite affirmative character is in the original motive, then it will reproduce its kind in forms of love, joy, strength and beauty with unerring precision. Before setting out, therefore, to produce new conditions by the exercise of our thought-power we should weigh carefully what further results they are likely to lead to; and here, again, we shall find an ample field for the training of our will, in learning to acquire that self-control which will enable us to postpone an inferior present satisfaction to a greater prospective good.

These considerations naturally lead us to the subject of concentration. I have just now pointed out that all duly controlled mental action consists in holding the mind in one of three attitudes; but there is a fourth mental condition, which is that of letting our mental functions run on without our will directing them to any definite purpose. It is on this word *purpose* that we must fix our whole attention; and instead of dissipating our energies, we must follow an intelligent method of concentration. The word means being gathered up at a centre, and the centre of anything is that point in which all its forces are equally balanced. To concentrate therefore means first to bring our minds into a condition of equilibrium which will enable us to consciously direct the flow of spirit to a definitely recognized purpose, and then carefully to guard our thoughts from inducing a flow in the opposite direction. We must always bear in mind that we are dealing with a wonderful *potential* energy which is not yet differentiated into any particular mode, and that by the action of our mind we can differentiate it into any specific mode of activity that we will; and by keeping our thought fixed on the fact that the inflow of this energy *is* taking place and that by our mental attitude we *are* determining its direction, we shall gradually realize a corresponding externalization. Proper concentration, therefore, does not consist of strenuous effort which exhausts the nervous system and defeats its own object by suggesting the consciousness of an adverse force to be fought against, and thus creating the adverse circumstances we dread; but in shutting out all thoughts of a kind that would disperse the spiritual nucleus we are forming and dwelling cheerfully on the knowledge that, because the law is certain in its action, our desire is certain of accomplishment. The other great principle to be remembered is that concentration is for the purpose of determining the *quality* we are going to give to the previously undifferentiated energy rather than to arrange the *specific circumstances* of its manifestation. *That* is the work of the creative energy itself, which will build up its own forms of expression quite naturally if we allow it, thus saving us a great deal of needless anxiety. What we really want is expansion in a certain direction, whether of health, wealth, or what not; and so long as we get this, what does it matter whether it reaches us through some channel which we thought we could reckon upon or through some other whose existence we had not suspected? It is the fact that we are concentrating energy of a particular kind for a particular purpose that we should fix our minds upon, and not look upon any specific details as essential to the accomplishment of our object.

These are the two golden rules regarding concentration; but we must not suppose that because we have to be on our guard against idle drifting there is to be no such thing as repose; on the contrary it is during periods of repose that we accumulate strength for action; but repose does not mean a state of purposelessness. As pure spirit the subjective mind never rests; it is only the objective mind in its connection with the physical body that needs rest; and though there are no doubt times when the greatest possible rest is to be obtained by stopping the action of our conscious thought altogether, the more generally advisable method is by changing the direction of the thought and, instead of centering it upon something we intend to *do*, letting it dwell quietly upon what we *are*. This direction of thought might, of course, develop into the deepest philosophical speculation, but it is not necessary that we should be always either consciously projecting our forces to produce some external effect or working out the details of some metaphysical problem; but we may simply realize ourselves as part of the universal livingness and thus gain a quiet centralization, which, though maintained by a conscious act of the volition, is the very essence of rest. From this standpoint we see that all is Life and all is Good, and that Nature, from her clearly visible surface to her most arcane depths, is one vast storehouse of life and good entirely devoted to our individual use. We have the key to all her treasures, and we can now apply our knowledge of the law of being without entering into all those details which are only needed for purposes of study, and doing so we find it results in our having acquired the consciousness of our *oneness with the whole*. This is the great secret; and when we have once fathomed it we can enjoy our possession of the whole, or of any part of it, because by our recognition we have made it, and can increasingly make it, our own. Whatever most appeals to us at any particular time or place is that mode of the universal living spirit with which at that moment we are most in touch, and realizing this, we shall draw from it streams of vital energy which will make the very sensation of livingness a joy and will radiate from us as a sphere of vibration that can deflect all injurious suggestion on whatever plane. We may not have literary, artistic, or scientific skill to present to others the results of our communings with Nature, but the joy of this sympathetic indrawing will nevertheless produce a corresponding outflow manifesting itself in the happier look and kindlier mien of him who thus realizes his oneness with every aspect of the whole. He realizes—and this is the great point in that attitude of mind which is not directed to any specific external object—that, for himself, he is and always must be the centre of all this galaxy of Life, and thus he contemplates himself as seated at the centre of infinitude, not an infinitude of blank space, but pulsating with living being, in all of which he knows that the true essence is nothing but good. This is the very opposite to a selfish self-centredness; it is the centre where we find that we both receive from all and flow out to all.

Apart from this principle of circulation there is no true life, and if we contemplate our central position only as affording us greater advantages for in-taking, we have missed the whole point of our studies by missing the real nature of the Life-principle, which is action and reaction. If we would have life enter into us, we ourselves must enter into life—enter into the spirit of it, just as we must enter into the spirit of a book or a game to enjoy it. There can be no action at a centre only. There must be a perpetual flowing out towards the circumference, and thence back again to the centre to maintain a vital activity; otherwise collapse must ensue either from anæmia or congestion. But if we realize the reciprocal nature of the vital pulsation, and that the outflowing consists in the habit of mind which gives itself to the good it sees in others, rather than in any specific actions, then we shall find that the cultivation of this disposition will provide innumerable avenues for the universal livingness to flow through us, whether as giving or receiving, which we had never before suspected; and this action and reaction will so build up our own vitality that each day will find us more thoroughly alive than any that had preceded it. This, then, is the attitude of repose in which we may enjoy all the beauties of science, literature and art or may peacefully commune with the spirit of nature without the aid of any third mind to act as its interpreter, which is still a purposeful attitude although not directed to a specific object; we have not allowed the will to relax its control, but have merely altered its direction; so that for action and repose alike we find that our strength lies in our recognition of the unity of the spirit and of ourselves as individual concentrations of it.

13

IN TOUCH WITH SUBCONSCIOUS MIND

THE PRECEDING pages have made the student in some measure aware of the immense importance of our dealings with the subconscious mind. Our relation to it, whether on the scale of the individual or the universal, is the key to all that we are or ever can be. In its unrecognized working it is the spring of all that we can call the automatic action of mind and body, and on the universal scale it is the silent power of evolution gradually working onwards to that "divine event, to which the whole creation moves"; and by our conscious recognition of it we make it, relatively to ourselves, all that we believe it to be. The closer our *rapport* with it becomes, the more what we have hitherto considered automatic action, whether in our bodies or our circumstances, will pass under our control, until at last we shall control our whole individual world. Since, then, this is the stupendous issue involved, the question how we are to put ourselves practically in touch with the subconscious mind is a very important one. Now the clue which gives us the right direction is to be found in the *impersonal* quality of subconscious mind of which I have spoken. Not impersonal as lacking the *elements* of personality; nor even, in the case of individual subjective mind, as lacking the sense of individuality; but impersonal in the sense of not recognizing the particular external relations which appear to the objective mind to constitute its personality, and having a realization of itself quite independent of them. If, then, we would come in touch with it we must meet it on its own ground. It can see things only from the deductive standpoint, and therefore cannot take note of the inductive standpoint from which we construct the idea of our external personality; and accordingly if we would put ourselves in touch with it, we cannot do so by bringing it down to the level of the external and nonessential but only by rising to its own level on the plane of the interior and essential. How can this be done? Let two well-known writers answer. Rudyard Kipling tells us in his story of "Kim" how the boy used at times to lose his sense of personality by repeating to himself the question, *Who* is Kim? Gradually his personality would seem to fade and he would experience a feeling of passing into a grander and a wider life, in which the boy Kim was unknown, while his own conscious individuality remained, only exalted and expanded to an inconceivable extent; and in Tennyson's life by his son we are told that at times the poet had a similar experience. We come into touch with the absolute exactly in proportion as we withdraw ourselves from the relative; they vary inversely to each other.

For the purpose, then, of getting into touch with our subconscious mind we must endeavour to think of ourselves as pure being, as that entity which interiorly supports the outward manifestation, and doing so we shall realize that the essential quality of pure being must be good. It is in itself *pure Life*, and as such cannot desire anything detrimental to pure Life under whatever form manifested. Consequently the purer our intentions the more readily we shall place ourself *en rapport* with our subjective entity; and *a fortiori* the same applies to that Greater Subconscious Mind of which our individual subjective mind is a particular manifestation. In actual practice the process consists in first forming a clear conception in the objective mind of the idea we wish to convey to the subjective mind; then, when this has been firmly grasped, endeavour to lose sight of all other facts connected with the external personality except the one in question, and then mentally address the subjective mind as though it were an independent entity and impress upon it what you want it to do or to believe. Everyone must formulate his own way of working, but one method, which is both simple and effective, is to say to the subjective mind, "This is what I want you to do; you will now step into my place and do it, bringing all your powers and intelligence to bear, and considering yourself to be none other than myself." Having done this, return to the realization of your own objective personality and leave the subjective mind to perform its task in full confidence that, by the law of its nature, it will do so if not hindered by a repetition of contrary messages from the objective mind. This is not a mere fancy but a truth daily proved by the experience of increasing numbers. The facts have not been fabricated to fit the theory, but the theory has been built up by careful observation of the facts; and since it has been shown both by theory and practice that such is the law of the relation between subjective and objective mind, we find ourselves face to face with a very momentous question. Is there any reason why the laws which hold good of the individual subjective mind should not hold good of the Universal Mind also? and the answer is that there is not. As has been already shown, the Universal Mind must, by its very universality, be purely subjective, and what is the law of a part must also be the law of the whole; the qualities of fire are the same whether the centres of combustion be great or small, and therefore we may well conclude these lectures by considering what will be the result if we apply what we have learnt regarding the individual subjective mind to the Universal Mind.

We have learnt that the three great facts regarding subjective mind are its creative power, its amenableness to suggestion, and its inability to work by any other than the deductive method. This last is an exceedingly important point, for it implies that the action of the subjective mind is in no way limited by precedent. The inductive method works on principles inferred from an already existing pattern, and therefore at the best only produces the old thing in a new shape. But the deductive method works according to the essence or spirit of the principle, and does not depend on any previous concrete manifestation for its apprehension of it; and this latter method of working must necessarily be that of the all-originating Mind, for since there could be no prior existing pattern from which it could learn the principles of construction, the want of a pattern would have prevented its creating anything had its method been inductive instead of deductive. Thus by the necessity of the case, the Universal Mind must act deductively, that is, according to the law which has been found true of individual subjective mind. It is thus not bound by any precedent, which means that its creative power is absolutely unlimited; and since it is essentially subjective mind, and not objective mind, it is entirely amenable to suggestion. Now it is an unavoidable inference from the identity of the law governing subjective mind, whether in the individual or the universal, that just as we can by suggestion impress a certain character of personality upon the individual subjective mind, so we can, and do, upon the Universal Mind; and it is for this reason that I have drawn attention to the inherent personal *quality* of pure spirit when contemplated in its most interior plane. It becomes, therefore, the most important of all considerations with what character we invest the Universal Mind; for since our relation to it is *purely subjective* it will infallibly bear *to us* exactly that character which we impress upon it; in other words it will be to us exactly what we believe it to be. This is simply a logical inference from the fact that, as subjective mind, our primary relation to it can only be on the subjective plane, and indirectly our objective relations must also spring from the same source. This is the meaning of that remarkable passage twice repeated in the Bible, "With the pure thou wilt show thyself pure, and with the froward thou wilt show thyself froward" (Ps. 18:26, and 2 Sam. 22:27), for the context makes it clear that these words are addressed to the Divine Being. The spiritual kingdom is *within* us, and as we realize it *there* so it becomes to us a reality. It is the unvarying law of the subjective life that "as a man thinketh in his heart so is he," that is to say, his inward subjective states are the only true reality, and what we call external realities are only their objective correspondences. If we thoroughly realize the truth that the Universal Mind must be to us exactly according to our conception of it, and that this relation is not merely imaginary but by the law of subjective mind must be to us an actual fact, and the foundation of all other facts, then it is impossible to overestimate the importance of the conception of the Universal Mind which we adopt. To the uninstructed there is little or no choice; they form a conception in accordance with the tradition they have received from others, and until they have learnt to think for themselves, they have to abide by the results of that tradition; for natural laws admit of no exceptions, and however faulty the traditional idea may be, its acceptance will involve a corresponding reaction upon the Universal Mind, which will in turn be reflected into the conscious mind and external life of the individual. But those who understand the law of the subject will have no one but themselves to blame if they do not derive all possible benefits from it. The greatest Teacher of Mental Science the world has ever seen has laid down sufficiently plain rules for our guidance. With a knowledge of the subject whose depth can be appreciated only by those who have themselves some practical acquaintance with it, He bids His unlearned audiences, those common people who heard Him gladly, picture to themselves the Universal Mind as a benign Father, tenderly compassionate of all and sending the common bounties of Nature alike on the evil and the good; but He also pictured It as exercising a special and peculiar care over those who recognize Its willingness to do so: "the very hairs of your head are all numbered," and "ye are of more value than many sparrows." Prayer was to be made to the unseen Being, not with doubt or fear, but with the absolute assurance of a certain answer, and no limit was to be set to its power or willingness to work for us. But to those who did not thus realize it, the Great Mind is necessarily the adversary who casts them into prison until they have paid the uttermost farthing; and thus in all cases the Master impressed upon his hearers the exact correspondence of the attitude of this unseen Power towards *them* with their own attitude towards *it*. Such teaching was not a narrow anthropomorphism but the adaptation to the intellectual capacity of the unlettered multitude of the very deepest truths of what we now call Mental Science. And the basis of it all is the cryptic personality of spirit hidden throughout the infinite of Nature under every form of manifestation. As unalloyed Life and Intelligence it *can* be no other than good, it can entertain no intention of evil, and thus all intentional evil must put us in opposition to it, and so deprive us of the consciousness of its guidance and strengthening and thus leave us to grope our own way and fight our own battle single-handed against the universe, odds which at last will surely prove too great for us. But remember that the opposition can never be on the part of the Universal Mind, for in itself it is subconscious mind; and to suppose any active opposition taken on its own initiative would be contrary to all we have learnt as to the nature of subconscious mind whether in the individual or the universal; the position of the Universal Mind towards us is always the reflection of our own attitude. Therefore although the Bible is full of threatening against those who persist in conscious opposition to the Divine Law of Good, it is on the other hand full of promises of immediate and full forgiveness to all who change their attitude and desire to cooperate with the Law of Good so far as they know it. The laws of Nature do not act vindictively; and through all theological formularies and traditional interpretations let us realize that what we are dealing with is the supreme law of our own being; and it is on the basis of this natural law that we find such declarations as that in Ezek. 18:22, which tells that if we forsake our evil ways our past transgressions shall never again be mentioned to us. We are dealing with the great principles of our subjective being, and our misuse of them in the past can never make them change their inherent law of action. If our method of using them in the past has brought us sorrow, fear and trouble, we have only to fall back on the law that if we reverse the cause the effects will be reversed also; and so what we have to do is simply to reverse our mental attitude and then endeavour to act up to the new one. The sincere endeavour to act up to our new mental attitude is essential, for we cannot really think in one way and act in another; but our repeated failures to fully act as we would wish must not discourage us. It is the sincere intention that is the essential thing, and this will in time release us from the bondage of habits which at present seem almost insuperable.

The initial step, then, consists in determining to picture the Universal Mind as the ideal of all we could wish it to be both to ourselves and to others, together with the endeavour to reproduce this ideal, however imperfectly, in our own life; and this step having been taken, we can then cheerfully look upon it as our ever-present Friend, providing all good, guarding from all danger, and guiding us with all counsel. Gradually as the habit of thus regarding the Universal Mind grows upon us, we shall find that in accordance with the laws we have been considering, it will become more and more *personal* to us, and in response to our desire its inherent intelligence will make itself more and more clearly perceptible within as a power of perceiving truth far beyond any statement of it that we could formulate by merely intellectual investigation. Similarly if we think of it as a great power devoted to supplying all our needs, we shall impress this character also upon it, and by the law of subjective mind it will proceed to enact the part of that special providence which we have credited it with being; and if, beyond the general care of our concerns, we would draw to ourselves some particular benefit, the same rule holds good of impressing our desire upon the Universal Subjective Mind. And if we realize that above and beyond all this we want something still greater and more enduring, the building-up of character and unfolding of our powers so that we may expand into fuller and yet fuller measures of joyous and joy-giving Life, still the same rule holds good: convey to the Universal Mind the suggestion of the desire, and by the law of relation between subjective and objective mind this too will be fulfilled. And thus the deepest problems of philosophy bring us back to the old statement of the Law: Ask and ye shall receive, seek and ye shall find, knock and it shall be opened unto you. This is the summing-up of the natural law of the relation between us and the Divine Mind. It is thus no vain boast that Mental Science can enable us to make our lives what we will. We must start from where we are now, and by rightly estimating our relation to the Divine Universal Mind we can gradually grow into any conditions we desire, provided we first make ourselves in habitual mental attitude the person who corresponds to those conditions; for we can never get over the law of correspondence, and the externalization will always be in accord with the internal principle that gives rise to it. And to this law there is no limit. What it can do for us today it can do tomorrow, and through all that procession of tomorrows that loses itself in the dim vistas of eternity. Belief in limitation is the one and only thing that causes limitation, because we thus impress limitation upon the creative principle; and in proportion as we lay that belief aside our boundaries will expand, and increasing life and more abundant blessing will be ours.

But we must not ignore our responsibilities. Trained thought is far more powerful than untrained, and therefore the more deeply we penetrate into Mental Science the more carefully we must guard against all thoughts and words expressive of even the most modified form of ill-will. Gossip, tale-bearing, sneering laughter, are not in accord with the principles of Mental Science; and similarly even our smallest thoughts of good carry with them a seed of good which will assuredly bear fruit in due time. This is not mere "goodie, goodie," but an important lesson in Mental Science, for our subjective mind takes its colour from our settled mental habits, and an occasional affirmation or denial will not be sufficient to change it; and we must therefore cultivate that tone which we wish to see reproduced in our conditions whether of body, mind, or circumstance.

In these lectures my purpose has been, not so much

to give specific rules of practice as to lay down the broad general principles of Mental Science which will enable the student to form rules for himself. In every walk in life, book knowledge is only a means to an end. Books can only direct us where to look and what to look for, but we must do the finding *for ourselves*; therefore, if you have really grasped the principles of the science, you will frame rules of your own which will give you better results than any attempt to follow somebody else's method, which was successful in their hands precisely because it was theirs. Never fear to be yourself. If Mental Science does not teach you to be yourself it teaches you nothing. Yourself, more yourself, and yet more yourself is what you want; only with the knowledge that the true self includes the inner and higher self which is always in immediate touch with the Great Divine Mind.

As Walt Whitman says: "You are not all included between your hat and your boots."

The growing popularity of the Edinburgh Lectures on Mental Science *has led me to add to the present edition three more sections on Body, Soul, and Spirit, which it is hoped will prove useful by rendering the principles of the interaction of these three factors somewhat clearer.*

14

THE BODY

SOME STUDENTS find it difficult to realize that mental action can produce any real effect upon material substance; but if this is not possible there is no such thing as Mental Science, the purpose of which is to produce improved conditions both of body and environment, so that the ultimate manifestation aimed at is always one of demonstration upon the plane of the visible and concrete. Therefore to afford conviction of an actual connection between the visible and the invisible, between the inner and the outer, is one of the most important points in the course of our studies.

That such a connection must exist is proved by metaphysical argument in answer to the question, "How did anything ever come into existence at all?" And the whole creation, ourselves included, stands as evidence to this great truth. But to many minds merely abstract argument is not completely convincing, or at any rate it becomes more convincing if it is supported by something of a more concrete nature; and for such readers I would give a few hints as to the correspondence between the physical and the mental.

The subject covers a very wide area, and the limited space at my disposal will only allow me to touch on a few suggestive points; still, these may be sufficient to show that the abstract argument has some corresponding facts at the back of it.

One of the most convincing proofs I have seen is that afforded by the "biometre," a little instrument invented by an eminent French scientist, the late Dr. Hippolyte Baraduc, which shows the action of what he calls the "vital current." His theory is that this force, whatever its actual nature may be, is universally present, and operates as a current of physical vitality perpetually, flowing with more or less energy through every physical organism, and which can, at any rate to some extent, be controlled by the power of the human will. The theory in all its minutiæ is exceedingly elaborate, and has been described in detail in Dr. Baraduc's published works. In a conversation I had with him about a year ago, he told me he was writing another book which would throw further light on the subject, but a few months later he passed over before it was presented to the world. The fact, however, which I wish to put before the reader, is the ocular demonstration of the connection between mind and matter, which an experiment with the biometre affords.

The instrument consists of a bell glass, from the inside of which is suspended a copper needle by a fine silken thread. The glass stands on a wooden support, below which is a coil of copper wire, which, however, is not connected with any battery or other apparatus, and merely serves to condense the current. Below the needle, inside the glass, there is a circular card divided into degrees to mark the action of the needle. Two of these instruments are placed side by side, but in no way connected, and the experimenter then holds out the fingers of both hands to within about an inch of the glasses. According to the theory, the current enters at the left hand, circulates through the body, and passes out at the right hand; that is to say, there is an indrawing at the left and a giving-out at the right, thus agreeing with Reichenbach's experiments on the polarity of the human body.

I must confess that, although I had read Dr. Baraduc's book, *Les Vibrations Humaines*, I approached the instrument in a very sceptical frame of mind; but I was soon convinced of my error. At first, holding a mental attitude of entire relaxation, I found that the left-hand needle was attracted through twenty degrees, while the right-hand needle, the one affected by the out-going current, was repelled through ten degrees. After allowing the instrument to return to its normal equilibrium I again approached it with the purpose of seeing whether a change of mental attitude would in the least modify the flow of current. This time I assumed the strongest mental attitude I could with the intention of sending out a flow through the right hand, and the result as compared with the previous one was remarkable. The left-hand needle was now attracted only through ten degrees, while the right-hand one was deflected through something over thirty, thus clearly indicating the influence of the mental faculties in modifying the action of the current. I may mention that the experiment was made in the presence of two medical men who noted the movement of the needles.

I will not here stop to discuss the question of what the actual constitution of this current of vital energy may be—it is sufficient for our present purpose that it is there, and the experiment I have described brings us face to face with the fact of a correspondence between our own mental attitude and the invisible forces of nature. Even if we say that this current is some form of electricity, and that the variation of its action is determined by changes in the polarization of the atoms of the body, then this change of polarity is the result of mental action; so that the quickening or retarding of the cosmic current is equally the result of the mental attitude whether we suppose our mental force to act directly upon the current itself or indirectly by inducing changes in the molecular structure of the body. Whichever hypothesis we adopt the conclusion is the same, namely, that the mind has power to open or close the door to invisible forces in such a way that the result of the mental action becomes apparent on the material plane.

Now, investigation shows that the physical body is a mechanism specially adapted for the transmutation of the inner or mental power into modes of external activity. We know from medical science that the whole body is traversed by a network of nerves which serve as the channels of communication between the indwelling spiritual ego, which we call mind, and the functions of the external organism. This nervous system is dual. One system, known as the Sympathetic, is the channel for all those activities which are not consciously directed by our volition, such as the operation of the digestive organs, the repair of the daily wear and tear of the tissues, and the like. The other system, known as the Voluntary or Cerebro-spinal system, is the channel through which we receive conscious perception from the physical senses and exercise control over the movements of the body. This system has its centre in the brain, while the other has its centre in a ganglionic mass at the back of the stomach known as the solar plexus, and sometimes spoken of as the abdominal brain. The cerebro-spinal system is the channel of our volitional or conscious mental action, and the sympathetic system is the channel of that mental action which unconsciously supports the vital functions of the body. Thus the cerebro-spinal system is the organ of conscious mind and the sympathetic is that of subconscious mind.

But the interaction of conscious and subconscious mind requires a similar interaction between the corresponding systems of nerves, and one conspicuous connection by which this is provided is the "vagus" nerve. This nerve passes out of the cerebral region as a portion of the voluntary system, and through it we control the vocal organs; then it passes onwards to the thorax sending out branches to the heart and lungs; and finally, passing through the diaphragm, it loses the outer coating which distinguishes the nerves of the voluntary system and becomes identified with those of the sympathetic system, so forming a connecting link between the two and making the man physically a single entity.

Similarly different areas of the brain indicate their connection with the objective and subjective activities of the mind respectively, and speaking in a general way we may assign the frontal portion of the brain to the former and the posterior portion to the latter, while the intermediate portion partakes of the character of both.

The intuitional faculty has its correspondence in this upper area of the brain situated between the frontal and posterior portions, and physiologically speaking, it is here that intuitive ideas find entrance. These at first are more or less unformed and generalized in character, but are nevertheless perceived by the conscious mind, otherwise we should not be aware of them at all. Then the effort of nature is to bring these ideas into more definite and usable shape, so the conscious mind lays hold of them and induces a corresponding vibratory current in the voluntary system of nerves, and this in turn induces a similar current in the involuntary system, thus handing the idea over to the subjective mind. The vibratory current which had first descended from the apex of the brain to the frontal brain and thus through the voluntary system to the solar plexus is now reversed and ascends from the solar plexus through the sympathetic system to the posterior brain, this return current indicating the action of the subjective mind.

If we were to remove the surface portion of the apex of the brain we should find immediately below it the shining belt of brain substance called the "corpus callosum." This is the point of union between the subjective and objective, and as the current returns from the solar plexus to this point it is restored to the objective portion of the brain in a fresh form which it has acquired by the silent alchemy of the subjective mind. Thus the conception which was at first only vaguely recognized is restored to the objective mind in a definite and workable form, and then the objective mind, acting through the frontal brain—the area of comparison and analysis—proceeds to work upon a clearly perceived idea and to bring out the potentialities that are latent in it.

It must of course be borne in mind that I am here speaking of the mental ego in that mode of its existence with which we are most familiar, that is as clothed in flesh, though there may be much to say as to other modes of its activity. But for our daily life we have to consider ourselves as we are in that aspect of life, and from this point of view the physiological correspondence of the body to the action of the mind is an important item; and therefore, although we must always remember that the origin of ideas is purely mental, we must not forget that on the physical plane every mental action implies a corresponding molecular action in the brain and in the twofold nervous system.

If, as the old Elizabethan poet says, "the soul is form, and doth the body make," then it is clear that the physical organism must be a mechanical arrangement as specially adapted for the use of the soul's powers as a steam-engine is for the power of steam; and it is the recognition of this reciprocity between the two that is the basis of all spiritual or mental healing, and therefore the study of this mechanical adaptation is an important branch of Mental Science. Only we must not forget that it is the effect and not the cause.

At the same time it is important to remember that such a thing as reversal of the relation between cause and effect is possible, just as the same apparatus may be made to generate mechanical power by the application of electricity, or to generate electricity by the application of mechanical power. And the importance of this principle consists in this. There is always a tendency for actions which were at first voluntary to become automatic, that is, to pass from the region of conscious mind into that of subconscious mind, and to acquire a permanent domicile there. Professor Elmer Gates, of Washington, has demonstrated this physiologically in his studies of brain formation. He tells us that every thought produces a slight molecular change in the substance of the brain, and the repetition of the same sort of thought causes a repetition of the same molecular action until at last a veritable channel is formed in the brain substance, which can only be eradicated by a reverse process of thought. In this way "grooves of thought" are very literal things, and when once established the vibrations of the cosmic currents flow automatically through them and thus react upon the mind by a process the reverse of that by which our voluntary and intentional indrawing from the invisible is effected. In this way are formed what we call "habits," and hence the importance of controlling our thinking and guarding it against undesirable ideas.

But on the other hand this reactionary process may be used to confirm good and life-giving modes of thought, so that by a knowledge of its laws we may enlist even the physical body itself in the building up of that perfectly whole personality, the attainment of which is the aim and object of our studies.

15

THE SOUL

Having now obtained a glimpse of the adaptation of the physical organism to the action of the mind, we must next realize that the mind itself is an organism which is in like manner adapted to the action of a still higher power, only here the adaptation is one of mental faculty. As with other invisible forces all we can know of the mind is by observing what it does, but with this difference: that since we ourselves *are* this mind, our observation is an interior observation of states of consciousness. In this way we recognize certain faculties of our mind, the working order of which I have considered at page 74; but the point to which I would now draw attention is that these faculties always work under the influence of something which stimulates them, and this stimulus may come either from without through the external senses, or from within by the consciousness of something not perceptible on the physical plane. Now the recognition of these interior sources of stimulus to our mental faculties is an important branch of Mental Science, because the mental action thus set up works just as accurately through the physical correspondences as those which start from the recognition of external facts, and therefore the control and right direction of these inner perceptions is a matter of the first moment.

The faculties most immediately concerned are the intuition and the imagination, but it is at first difficult to see how the intuition, which is entirely spontaneous, can be brought under the control of the will. Of course, the spontaneousness of the intuition cannot in any way be interfered with, for if it ceased to act spontaneously it would cease to be the intuition. Its province is, as it were, to capture ideas from the infinite and present them to the mind to be dealt with at its discretion. In our mental constitution the intuition is the point of origination and, therefore, for it to cease to act spontaneously would be for it to cease to act at all. But the experience of a long succession of observers shows that the intuition can be trained so as to acquire increased sensitiveness in some particular direction, and the choice of the *general direction* is determined by the will of the individual.

It will be found that the intuition works most readily in respect to those subjects which most habitually occupy our thought; and according to the physiological correspondences which we have been considering, this might be accounted for on the physical plane by the formation of brain-channels specially adapted for the induction in the molecular system of vibrations corresponding to the particular class of ideas in question. But of course we must remember that the ideas themselves are not caused by the molecular changes, but on the contrary are the cause of them; and it is in this translation of thought action into physical action that we are brought face to face with the eternal mystery of the descent of spirit into matter; and that though we may trace matter through successive degrees of refinement till it becomes what, in comparison with those denser modes that are most familiar, we might call a spiritual substance, yet at the end of it, it is not the intelligent thinking principle itself. The criterion is in the word "vibrations." However delicately etheric the substance, its movement commences by the vibration of its particles, and a vibration is a wave having a certain length, amplitude, and periodicity, that is to say, something which can exist only in terms of space and time; and as soon as we are dealing with anything capable of the conception of measurement we may be quite certain that we are not dealing with Spirit but only with one of its vehicles. Therefore although we may push our analysis of matter further and ever further back—and on this line there is a great deal of knowledge to be gained—we shall find that the point at which spiritual power or thought-force is translated into etheric or atomic vibration will always elude us. Therefore we must not attribute the origination of ideas to molecular displacement in the brain, though, by the reaction of the physical upon the mental which I have spoken of above, the formation of thought-channels in the grey matter of the brain may tend to facilitate the reception of certain ideas. Some people are actually conscious of the action of the upper portion of the brain during the influx of an intuition, the sensation being that of a sort of expansion in that brain area, which might be compared to the opening of a valve or door; but all attempts to induce the inflow of intuitive ideas by the physiological expedient of trying to open this valve by the exercise of the will should be discouraged as likely to prove injurious to the brain. I believe some Oriental systems advocate this method, but we may well trust the mind to regulate the action of its physical channels in a manner suitable to its own requirements, instead of trying to manipulate the mind by the unnatural forcing of its mechanical instrument. In all our studies on these lines we must remember that development is always by perfectly natural growth and is not brought about by unduly straining any portion of the system.

The fact, however, remains that the intuition works most freely in that direction in which we most habitually concentrate our thought; and in practice it will be found that the best way to cultivate the intuition in any particular direction is to meditate upon the *abstract principles* of that particular class of subjects rather than only to consider particular cases. Perhaps the reason is that particular cases have to do with specific phenomena, that is with the law working under certain limiting conditions, whereas the *principles* of the law are not limited by local conditions, and so habitual meditation on *them* sets our intuition free to range in an infinitude where the conception of antecedent conditions does not limit it. Anyway, whatever may be the theoretical explanation, you will find that the clear grasp of abstract principles in any direction has a wonderfully quickening effect upon the intuition in that particular direction.

The importance of recognizing our power of thus giving direction to the intuition cannot be exaggerated, for if the mind is attuned to sympathy with the highest phases of spirit this power opens the door to limitless possibilities of knowledge. In its highest workings intuition becomes inspiration, and certain great records of fundamental truths and supreme mysteries which have come down to us from thousands of generations bequeathed by deep thinkers of old can only be accounted for on the supposition that their earnest thought on the Originating Spirit, coupled with a reverent worship of It, opened the door, through their intuitive faculty, to the most sublime inspirations regarding the supreme truths of the universe both with respect to the evolution of the cosmos and to the evolution of the individual. Among such records explanatory of the supreme mysteries three stand out pre-eminent, all bearing witness to the same ONE Truth, and each throwing light upon the other; and these three are the Bible, the Great Pyramid, and the Pack of Cards—a curious combination some will think, but I hope in another volume of this series to be able to justify my present statement. I allude to these three records here because the unity of principle which they exhibit, notwithstanding their wide divergence of method, affords a standing proof that the direction taken by the intuition is largely determined by the will of the individual opening the mind in that particular direction.

Very closely allied to the intuition is the faculty of imagination. This does not mean mere fancies, which we dismiss without further consideration, but our power of forming mental images upon which we dwell. These, as I have said in the earlier part of this book, form a nucleus which, on its own plane, calls into action the universal Law of Attraction, thus giving rise to the principle of Growth. The relation of the intuition to the imagination is that the intuition grasps an idea from the Great Universal Mind, in which all things subsist *as potentials*, and presents it to the imagination in its essence rather than in a definite form, and then our image-building faculty gives it a clear and definite form which it presents before the mental vision, and which we then vivify by letting our thought dwell upon it, thus infusing our own personality into it, and so providing that personal element through which the specific action of the universal law relatively to the particular individual always takes place.* Whether our thought shall be allowed thus to dwell upon a particular mental image depends on our own will, and our exercise of our will depends on our belief in our power to use it so as to disperse or consolidate a given mental image; and finally our belief in our power to do this depends on our recognition of our relation to God, Who is the source of all power; for it is an invariable truth that our life will take its whole form, tone, and color from our conception of God, whether that conception be positive or negative, and the sequence by which it does so is that now given.

In this way, then, our intuition is related to our imagination, and this relation has its physiological correspondence in the circulus of molecular vibrations I have described above, which, having its commencement in the higher or "ideal" portion of the brain, flows through the voluntary nervous system, the physical channel of objective mind, returning through the sympathetic system, the physical channel of subjective mind, thus completing the circuit and being then restored to the frontal brain, where it is consciously

*See my *Doré Lectures*.

modelled into clear-cut forms suited to a specific purpose.

In all this the power of the will as regulating the action both of the intuition and the imagination must never be lost sight of, for without such a central controlling power we should lose all sense of individuality; and hence the ultimate aim of the evolutionary process is to evolve individual wills actuated by such beneficence and enlightenment as shall make them fitting vehicles for the outflowing of the Supreme Spirit, which has hitherto created cosmically, and can now carry on the creative process to its highest stages only through conscious union with the individual; for this is the only possible solution of the great problem, How can the Universal Mind act in all its fulness upon the plane of the individual and particular?

This is the ultimate of evolution, and the successful evolution of the individual depends on his recognizing this ultimate and working towards it; and therefore this should be the great end of our studies. There is a correspondence in the constitution of the body to the faculties of the soul, and there is a similar correspondence in the faculties of the soul to the power of the All-originating Spirit; and as in all other adaptations of specific vehicles so also here, we can never correctly understand the nature of the vehicle and use it rightly until we realize the nature of the power for the working of which it is specially adapted. Let us, then, in conclusion briefly consider the nature of that power.

16

THE SPIRIT

WHAT MUST the Supreme All-originating Spirit be in itself? That is the question before us. Let us start with one fact regarding it about which we cannot have any possible doubt—it is *creative*. If it were not creative nothing could come into existence; therefore we know that its purpose, or Law of Tendency, must be to bring individual lives into existence and to surround them with a suitable environment. Now a power which has this for its inherent nature must be a kindly power. The Spirit of Life seeking expression in individual lives can have no other intention towards them than "that they might have life, and that they might have it more abundantly." To suppose the opposite would be a contradiction in terms. It would be to suppose the Eternal Principle of Life acting against itself, expressing itself as the reverse of what it is, in which case it would not be expressing itself but expressing its opposite; so that it is impossible to conceive of the Spirit of Life acting otherwise than to the increase of life. This is as yet only imperfectly apparent by reason of our imperfect apprehension of the position, and our consequent want of conscious unity with the ONE Eternal Life. As our consciousness of unity becomes more perfect so will the life-givingness of the Spirit become more apparent. But in the realm of principles the purely Affirmative and Life-giving nature of the All-originating Spirit is an unavoidable conclusion. Now by what name can we call such an inherent desire to add to the fulness of any individual life—that is, to make it stronger, brighter, and happier? If this is not Love, then I do not know what else it is; and so we are philosophically led to the conclusion that Love is the prime moving power of the Creating Spirit.

But expression is impossible without Form. What Form, then, should Love give to the vehicles of its expression? By the hypothesis of the case, it could not find self-expression in forms that were hateful or repugnant to it—therefore the only logical correlative of Love is Beauty. Beauty is not yet universally manifested for the same reason that Life is not, namely, lack of recognition of its Principle; but, that the principle of Beauty is inherent in the Eternal Mind is demonstrated by all that is beautiful in the world in which we live.

These considerations show us that the inherent nature of the Spirit must consist in the eternal interaction of Love and Beauty as the Active and Passive polarity of Being. Then this is the Power for the working of which our soul faculties are specially adapted. And when this purpose of the adaptation is recognized we begin to get some insight into the way in which our intuition, imagination, and will should be exercised. By training our thought to habitually dwell upon this dual-unity of the Originating Forces of Love and Beauty the intuition is rendered more and more sensitive to ideas emanating from this supreme source, and the imagining faculty is trained in the formation of images corresponding to such ideas; while on the physical side the molecular structure of the brain and body becomes more and more perfectly adjusted to the generating of vibratory currents tending to the outward manifestation of the Originating Principle. Thus the whole man is brought into unison with himself and with the Supreme Source of Life, so that, in the words of St. Paul, he is being day by day renewed after the image of Him that created him.

Our more immediately personal recognition of the All-originating Love and Beauty will thus flow out as peace of mind, health of body, discretion in the management of our affairs, and power in the carrying out of our undertakings; and as we advance to a wider conception of the working of the Spirit of Love and Beauty in its infinite possibilities, so our intuition will find a wider scope and our field of activity will expand along with it – in a word, we shall discover that our individuality is growing, and that we are becoming more truly ourselves than we ever were before.

The question of the specific lines on which the individual may be most perfectly trained into such recognition of his true relation to the All-embracing Spirit of Life is therefore of supreme importance, but it is also of such magnitude that even to briefly sketch its broad outlines would require a volume to itself, and I will therefore not attempt to enter upon it here, my present purpose being only to offer some hints of the principles underlying that wonderful three-fold unity of Body, Soul, and Spirit which we all know ourselves to be.

We are as yet only at the commencement of the path which leads to the realization of this unity in the full development of all its powers, but others have trodden the way before us, from whose experiences we may learn; and not least among these was the illustrious founder of the Most Christian Fraternity of the Rosicrucians. This master-mind, setting out in his youth with the intention of going to Jerusalem, changed the order of his journey and first sojourned for three years in the symbolical city of Damcar, in the mystical country of Arabia, then for about a year in the mystical country of Egypt, and then for two years in the mystical country of Fez. Then, having during these six years learned all that was to be acquired in those countries, he returned to his native land of Germany, where, on the basis of the knowledge he had thus gained, he founded the Fraternity R. C., for whose instruction he wrote the mystical books M. and T. Then, when he realized that his work in its present stage was accomplished, he of his own free will laid aside the physical body, not, it is recorded, by decay, or disease, or ordinary death, but by the express direction of the Spirit of Life, summing up all his knowledge in the words

Jesus mihi omnia.

And now his followers await the coming of "the Artist Elias," who shall bring the Magnum Opus to its completion.

"Let him that readeth understand."

THE DORÉ LECTURES ON MENTAL SCIENCE

FOREWORD

The addresses contained in this volume were delivered by me at the Doré Gallery, Bond Street, London, on the Sundays of the first three months of the present year, and are now published at the kind request of many of my hearers, hence their title of *The Doré Lectures.* A number of separate discourses on a variety of subjects necessarily labours under the disadvantage of want of continuity, and also under that of a liability to the frequent repetition of similar ideas and expressions, and the reader will, I trust, pardon these defects as inherent in the circumstances of the work. At the same time it will be found that, although not specially so designed, there is a certain progressive development of thought through the dozen lectures which compose this volume, the reason for which is that they all aim at expressing the same fundamental idea, namely that, though the laws of the universe can never be broken, they can be made to work under special conditions which will produce results that could not be produced under the conditions spontaneously provided by nature. This is a simple scientific principle and it shows us the place which is occupied by the personal factor, that, namely, of an intelligence which sees beyond the present limited manifestation of the Law into its real essence, and which thus constitutes the instrumentality by which the infinite possibilities of the Law can be evoked into forms of power, usefulness, and beauty.

The more perfect, therefore, the working of the personal factor, the greater will be the results developed from the Universal Law; and hence our lines of study should be twofold – on the one hand the theoretical study of the action of Universal Law, and on the other the practical fitting of ourselves to make use of it; and if the present volume should assist any reader in this twofold quest, it will have answered its purpose.

The different subjects have necessarily been treated very briefly, and the addresses can only be considered as suggestions for lines of thought which the reader will be able to work out for himself, and he must therefore not expect that careful elaboration of detail which I would gladly have bestowed had I been writing on one of these subjects exclusively. This little book must be taken only for what it is, the record of somewhat fragmentary talks with a very indulgent audience, to whom I gratefully dedicate the volume.

T. T.

June 5, 1909

1

ENTERING INTO THE SPIRIT OF IT

We all know the meaning of this phrase in our everyday life. The Spirit is that which gives life and movement to anything, in fact it is that which causes it to exist at all. The thought of the author, the impression of the painter, the feeling of the musician, is that without which their works could never have come into being, and so it is only as we enter into the *idea* which gives rise to the work, that we can derive all the enjoyment and benefit from it which it is able to bestow. If we cannot enter into the Spirit of it, the book, the picture, the music, are meaningless to us; to appreciate them we must share the mental attitude of their creator. This is a universal principle; if we do not enter into the Spirit of a thing, it is dead so far as we are concerned; but if we do enter into it we reproduce in ourselves the same quality of life which called that thing into existence.

Now if this is a general principle, why can we not carry it to a higher range of things? Why not to the highest point of all? May we not enter into the originating Spirit of Life itself, and so reproduce it in ourselves as a perennial spring of livingness? This, surely, is a question worthy of our careful consideration.

The spirit of a thing is that which is the source of its inherent movement, and therefore the question before us is, what is the nature of the primal moving power, which is at the back of the endless array of life which we see around us, our own life included? Science gives us ample ground for saying that it is not material, for science has now, at least theoretically, reduced all material things to a primary ether, universally distributed, whose innumerable particles are in absolute equilibrium; whence it follows on mathematical grounds alone that the initial movement which began to concentrate the world and all material substances out of the particles of the dispersed ether, could not have originated in the particles themselves. Thus by a necessary deduction from the conclusions of physical science, we are compelled to realize the presence of some immaterial power capable of separating off certain specific areas for the display of cosmic activity, and then building up a material universe with all its inhabitants by an orderly sequence of evolution, in which each stage lays the foundation for the development of the stage which is to follow — in a word we find ourselves brought face to face with a power which exhibits on a stupendous scale, the faculties of selection and adaptation of means to ends, and thus distributes energy and life in accordance with a recognizable scheme of cosmic progression. It is therefore not only Life, but also Intelligence, and Life guided by Intelligence becomes Volition. It is this primary originating power which we mean when we speak of "The Spirit," and it is into this Spirit of the whole universe that we must enter if we would reproduce it as a spring of Original Life in ourselves.

Now in the case of the productions of artistic genius we know that we must enter into the movement of the creative mind of the artist, before we can realize the principle which gives rise to his work. We must learn to partake of the feeling, to find expression for which is the motive of his creative activity. May we not apply the same principle to the Greater Creative Mind with which we are seeking to deal? There is something in the work of the artist which is akin to that of original creation. His work, literary, musical, or graphic is original creation on a miniature scale, and in this it differs from that of the engineer, which is constructive, or that of the scientist which is analytical; for the artist in a sense creates something out of nothing, and therefore starts from the standpoint of simple feeling, and not from that of a pre-existing necessity. This, by the hypothesis of the case, is true also of the Parent Mind, for at the stage where the initial movement of creation takes place, there are no existing conditions to compel action in one direction more than another. Consequently the direction taken by the creative impulse is not dictated by outward circumstances, and the primary movement must therefore be entirely due to the action of the Original Mind upon itself; it is the reaching out of this Mind for realization of all that it feels itself to be.

The creative process thus in the first instance is purely a matter of feeling—exactly what we speak of as "motif" in a work of art.

Now it is this original feeling that we need to enter into, because it is the *fons et origo* of the whole chain of causation which subsequently follows. What then can this original feeling of the Spirit be? Since the

Spirit is Life-in-itself, its feeling can only be for the fuller expression of Life—any other sort of feeling would be self-destructive and is therefore inconceivable. Then the full expression of Life implies Happiness, and Happiness implies Harmony, and Harmony implies Order, and Order implies Proportion, and Proportion implies Beauty; so that in recognizing the inherent tendency of the Spirit towards the production of Life, we can recognise a similar inherent tendency to the production of these other qualities also; and since the desire to bestow the greater fulness of joyous life can only be described as Love, we can sum up the whole of the feeling which is the original moving impulse in the Spirit as Love and Beauty—the Spirit finding expression through forms of beauty in centres of life, in harmonious reciprocal relation to itself. This is a generalized statement of the broad principle by which Spirit expands from the innermost to the outermost, in accordance with a Law of tendency inherent in itself.

It sees itself, as it were, reflected in various centres of life and energy, each with its appropriate form; but in the first instance these reflections can have no existence except within the originating Mind. They have their first beginning as mental images, so that in addition to the powers of Intelligence and Selection, we must also realise that of Imagination as belonging to the Divine Mind; and we must picture these powers as working from the initial motive of Love and Beauty.

Now this is the Spirit that we need to enter into, and the method of doing so is a perfectly logical one. It is the same method by which all scientific advance is made. It consists in first observing how a certain law works under the conditions spontaneously provided by nature, next in carefully considering what principle this spontaneous working indicates, and lastly deducing from this how the same principle would act under specially selected conditions, not spontaneously provided by nature.

The progress of shipbuilding affords a good example of what I mean. Formerly wood was employed instead of iron, because wood floats in water and iron sinks; yet now the navies of the world are built of iron; careful thought showed the law of flotation to be that anything could float which, bulk for bulk, is lighter than the mass of liquid displaced by it; and so we now make iron float by the very same law by which it sinks, because by the introduction of the *personal* factor, we provide conditions which do not occur spontaneously —according to the esoteric maxim that "Nature unaided fails." Now we want to apply the same process of specializing a generic Law to the first of all Laws, that of the generic life-giving tendency of Spirit itself. Without the element of *individual personality* the Spirit can only work cosmically by a *generic* Law; but this law admits of far higher specialization, and this specialization can only be attained through the introduction of the personal factor. But to introduce this factor the individual must be fully aware of the *principle* which underlies the spontaneous or cosmic action of the law. Where, then, will he find this principle of Life? Certainly not by contemplating Death. In order to get a principle to work in the way we require it to, we must observe its action when it is working spontaneously in this particular direction. We must ask why it goes in the right direction as far as it does—and having learnt this we shall then be able to make it go further. The law of flotation was not discovered by contemplating the sinking of things, but by contemplating the floating of things which floated naturally, and then intelligently asking why they did so.

The knowledge of a principle is to be gained by the study of its affirmative action; when we understand *that* we are in a position to correct the negative conditions which tend to prevent that action.

Now Death is the absence of Life, and disease is the absence of health, so to enter into the Spirit of Life we require to contemplate it, where it is to be found, and not where it is not—we are met with the old question, "Why seek ye the living among the dead?" This is why we start our studies by considering the cosmic creation, for it is there that we find the Life Spirit working through untold ages, not merely as deathless energy, but with a perpetual advance into higher degrees of Life. If we could only so enter into the Spirit as to make it personally *in ourselves* what it evidently is in *itself*, the *magnum opus* would be accomplished. This means realizing our life as drawn direct from the Originating Spirit; and if we now understand that the Thought or Imagination of the Spirit is the great reality of Being, and that all material facts are only correspondences, then it logically follows that what we have to do is to maintain our individual place in the Thought of the Parent Mind.

We have seen that the action of the Originating Mind must needs be *generic*, that is according to types which include multitudes of individuals. This type is the reflection of the Creative Mind at the level of that particular *genus*; and at the human level it is Man, not as associated with particular circumstances, but as existing in the absolute ideal.

In proportion then as we learn to dissociate our conception of ourselves from particular circumstances, and to rest upon our *absolute* nature, as reflections of the Divine ideal, we, in our turn, reflect back into the Divine Imagination its original conception of itself as expressed in generic or typical Man, and so by a natural law of cause and effect, the individual who realizes this mental attitude enters permanently into the Spirit of Life, and it becomes a perennial fountain of Life springing up spontaneously within him.

He then finds himself to be as the Bible says, "the image and likeness of God." He has reached the level at which he affords a new starting point for the creative process, and the Spirit, finding a personal centre in him, begins its work *de novo*, having thus solved the great problem of how to enable the Universal to act directly upon the plane of the Particular.

It is in this sense, as affording the requisite centre for a new departure of the creative Spirit, that man is said to be a "microcosm," or universe in miniature; and this is also what is meant by the esoteric doctrine of the Octave, of which I may be able to speak more fully on some other occasion.

If the principles here stated are carefully considered, they will be found to throw light on much that would otherwise be obscure, and they will also afford the key to the succeeding essays.

The reader is therefore asked to think them out carefully for himself, and to note their connection with the subject of the next article.

2

INDIVIDUALITY

Individuality is the necessary complement of the Universal Spirit, which was the subject of our consideration last Sunday. The whole problem of life consists in finding the true relation of the individual to the Universal Originating Spirit; and the first step towards ascertaining this is to realize what the Universal Spirit must be in itself. We have already done this to some extent, and the conclusions we have arrived at are:

That the essence of the Spirit is Life, Love, and Beauty.

That its Motive, or primary moving impulse, is to express the Life, Love and Beauty which it feels itself to be.

That the Universal cannot act on the plane of the Particular except by becoming the particular, that is, by expression through the individual.

If these three axioms are clearly grasped, we have got a solid foundation from which to start our consideration of the subject for today.

The first question that naturally presents itself is,

If these things be so, why does not every individual express the life, love, and beauty of the Universal Spirit? The answer to this question is to be found in the Law of Consciousness. We cannot be conscious of anything except by realizing a certain relation between it and ourselves. It must affect us in some way, otherwise we are not conscious of its existence; and according to the way in which it affects us we recognize ourselves as standing related to it. It is this self-recognition on our own part carried out to the sum total of all our relations, whether spiritual, intellectual, or physical, that constitutes our realization of life. On this principle, then, for the *realization* of its own Livingness, the production of centres of life, through its relation to which this conscious realization can be attained, becomes a necessity for the Originating Mind. Then it follows that this realization can only be complete where the individual has perfect liberty to withhold it; for otherwise no true realization could have taken place. For instance, let us consider the working of Love. Love must be spontaneous, or it has no existence at all. We cannot imagine such a thing as mechanically induced love. But anything which is formed so as to automatically produce an effect without any volition of its own, is nothing but a piece of mechanism. Hence if the Originating Mind is to realize the reality of Love, it can only be by relation to some being which has the power to withhold love. The same applies to the realization of all the other modes of livingness; so that it is only in proportion as the individual life is an independent centre of action, with the option of acting either positively or negatively, that any real life has been produced at all. The further the created thing is from being a merely mechanical arrangement, the higher is the grade of creation. The solar system is a perfect work of mechanical creation, but to constitute centres which can reciprocate the highest nature of the Divine Mind requires not a mechanism, however perfect, but a mental centre which is, in itself, an independent source of action. Hence by the requirements of the case man should be capable of placing himself either in a positive or a negative relation to the Parent Mind, from which he originates; otherwise he would be nothing more than a clockwork figure.

In this necessity of the case, then, we find the reason why the life, love, and beauty of the Spirit are not visibly reproduced in every human being. They *are* reproduced in the world of nature, so far as a mechanical and automatic action can represent them, but their perfect reproduction can only take place on the basis of a liberty akin to that of the Originating Spirit itself, which therefore implies the liberty of negation as well as of affirmation.

Why, then, does the individual make a negative choice? Because he does not understand the law of his own individuality, and believes it to be a law of limitation, instead of a Law of Liberty. He does not expect to find the starting point of the Creative Process reproduced within himself, and so he looks to the mechanical side of things for the basis of his reasoning about life. Consequently his reasoning lands him in the conclusion that life is limited, because he has assumed limitation in his premises, and so logically cannot escape from it in his conclusion. Then he thinks that this is the law and so ridicules the idea of transcending it. He points to the sequence of cause and effect, by which death, disease, and disaster hold their sway over the individual, and says that sequence is law. And he is perfectly right so far as he goes—it is *a* law; but not *the* Law. When we have only reached this stage of comprehension, we have yet to learn that a higher law can include a lower one so completely as entirely to swallow it up.

The fallacy involved in this negative argument, is the assumption that the law of limitation is essential in all grades of being. It is the fallacy of the old shipbuilders as to the impossibility of building iron ships. What is required is to get at the *principle* which is at the back of the Law in its affirmative working, and specialize it under higher conditions than are spontaneously presented by nature, and this can only be done by the introduction of the personal element, that is to say an individual intelligence capable of comprehending the principle. The question, then, is, what is the principle by which we came into being? and this is only a personal application of the general question, How did anything come into being? Now, as I pointed out in the preceding article, the ultimate deduction from physical science is that the originating movement takes place in the Universal Mind, and is analogous to that of our own imagination; and as we have just seen, the perfect ideal can only be that of a being capable of reciprocating *all* the qualities of the Originating Mind. Consequently man, in his inmost nature, is the product of the Divine Mind imaging forth an image of itself on the plane of the relative as the complementary to its own sphere of the absolute.

If we will therefore go to the *inmost* principle in

ourselves, which philosophy and Scripture alike declare to be made in the image and likeness of God, instead of to the outer vehicles which it externalizes as instruments through which to function on the various planes of being, we shall find that we have reached a principle in ourselves which stands in *loco dei* towards all our vehicles and also towards our environment. It is above them all, and creates them, however unaware we may be of the fact, and relatively to them it occupies the place of first cause. The recognition of this is the discovery of our own relation to the whole world of the relative. On the other hand this must not lead us into the mistake of supposing that there is nothing higher, for, as we have already seen, this inmost principle or *ego* is itself the effect of an antecedent cause, for it proceeds from the imaging process in the Divine Mind.

We thus find ourselves holding an intermediate position between true First Cause, on the one hand, and the world of secondary causes on the other, and in order to understand the nature of this position, we must fall back on the axiom that the Universal can only work on the plane of the Particular through the individual. Then we see that the function of the individual is to *differentiate* the undistributed flow of the Universal into suitable directions for starting different trains of secondary causation.

Man's place in the cosmic order is that of a distributor of the Divine power, subject, however, to the inherent Law of the power which he distributes. We see one instance of this in ordinary science, in the fact that we never create force; all we can do is to distribute it. The very word Man means distributor or measurer, as in common with all words derived from the

Sanskrit root MN., it implies the idea of measurement, just as in the words moon, month, mens, mind, and "man," the Indian weight of 80 lbs.; and it is for this reason that man is spoken of in Scripture as a "steward," or dispenser of the Divine gifts. As our minds become open to the full meaning of this position, the immense possibilities and also the responsibility contained in it will become apparent.

It means that the individual is the creative centre of his own world. Our past experience affords no evidence against this, but on the contrary, is evidence for it. Our true nature is always present, only we have hitherto taken the lower and mechanical side of things for our starting point, and so have created limitation instead of expansion. And even with the knowledge of the Creative Law which we have now attained, we shall continue to do this, if we seek our starting point in the things which are below us and not in the only thing which is above us, namely the Divine Mind, because it is only there that we can find illimitable Creative Power. Life is *being*, it is the experience of states of consciousness, and there is an unfailing correspondence between these inner states and our outward conditions. Now we see from the Original Creation that the state of consciousness must be the cause, and the corresponding conditions the effect, because at the starting of the creation no conditions existed, and the working of the Creative Mind upon itself can only have been a state of consciousness. This, then, is clearly the Creative Order—from states to conditions. But we invert this order, and seek to create from conditions to states. We say, If I had such and such conditions they would produce the state of feeling which I desire; and in so saying we run the risk of making a mistake as to the correspondence, for it may turn out that the particular conditions which we fixed on are not such as would produce the desired state. Or, again, though they might produce it in a certain degree, other conditions might produce it in a still greater degree, while at the same time opening the way to the attainment of still higher states and still better conditions. Therefore our wisest plan is to follow the pattern of the Parent Mind and make mental self-recognition our starting point, knowing that by the inherent Law of Spirit the correlated conditions will come by a natural process of growth. Then the great self-recognition is that of our relation to the Supreme Mind. That is the generating centre and we are distributing centres; just as electricity is generated at the central station and delivered in different forms of power by reason of passing through appropriate centres of distribution, so that in one place it lights a room, in another conveys a message, and in a third drives a tram car. In like manner the power of the Universal Mind takes particular forms through the particular mind of the individual. It does not interfere with the lines of his individuality, but works along them, thus making him, not less, but more himself. It is thus, not a compelling power, but an expanding and illuminating one; so that the more the individual recognizes the reciprocal action between it and himself, the more full of life he must become.

Then also we need not be troubled about future conditions because we know that the All-originating Power is working through us and for us, and that according to the Law proved by the whole existing creation, it produces all the conditions required for the expression of the Life, Love and Beauty which it is, so that we can fully trust it to open the way as we go along. The Great Teacher's words, "Take no thought for the morrow"—and note that the correct translation is "Take no anxious thought"—are the practical application of the soundest philosophy. This does not, of course, mean that we are not to exert ourselves. We must do our share in the work, and not expect God to do *for* us what He can only do *through* us. We are to use our common sense and natural faculties in working upon the conditions now present. We must make use of them, *as far as they go,* but we must not try and go further than the present things require; we must not try to force things, but allow them to grow naturally, knowing that they are doing so under the guidance of the All-Creating Wisdom.

Following this method we shall grow more and more into the habit of looking to mental attitude as the Key to our progress in Life, knowing that everything else must come out of that; and we shall further discover that our mental attitude is eventually determined by the way in which we regard the Divine Mind. Then the final result will be that we shall see the Divine Mind to be nothing else than Life, Love and Beauty—Beauty being identical with Wisdom or the perfect adjustment of parts to whole—and we shall see ourselves to be distributing centres of these primary energies and so in our turn subordinate centres of creative power. And as we advance in this knowledge we shall find that we transcend one law of limitation after another by finding the higher law, of which the lower is but a partial expression, until we shall see clearly before us, as our ultimate goal, nothing less than the Perfect Law of Liberty—not liberty without Law which is anarchy, but Liberty according to Law. In this way we shall find that the Apostle spoke the literal truth, when he said that we shall become like Him when we see Him *as He is*, because the whole process by which our individuality is produced is one of reflection of the image existing in the Divine Mind. When we thus learn the Law of our own being we shall be able to specialize it in ways of which we have hitherto but little conception, but as in the case of all natural laws the specialization cannot take place until the fundamental principle of the generic law has been fully realized. For these reasons the student should endeavour to realize more and more perfectly, both in theory and practice, the law of the relation between the Universal and the Individual Minds. It is that of *reciprocal* action. If this fact of reciprocity is grasped, it will be found to explain both why the individual falls short of expressing the fulness of Life, which the Spirit is, and why he can attain to the fulness of that expression; just as the same law explains why iron sinks in water, and how it can be made to float. It is the individualizing of the Universal Spirit, by recognizing its reciprocity to ourselves, that is the secret of the perpetuation and growth of our own individuality.

3

THE NEW THOUGHT AND THE NEW ORDER

IN THE TWO preceding lectures I have endeavoured to reach some conception of what the All-originating Spirit is in itself, and of the relation of the individual to it. So far as we can form any conception of these things at all we see that they are universal principles applicable to all nature, and, at the human level, applicable to all men; they are general laws the recognition of which is an essential preliminary to any further advance, because progress is made, not by setting aside the inherent law of things, which is impossible, but by specializing it through presenting conditions which will enable the same principle to act in a less limited manner. Having therefore got a general idea of these two ultimates, the universal and the individual, and of their relation to one another, let us now consider the process of specialization. In what does the specialization of a natural law consist? It consists in making that law or principle produce an effect which it could not produce under the simply generic conditions spontaneously provided by nature.

This selection of suitable conditions is the work of Intelligence, it is a process of consciously arranging things in a new order, so as to produce a new result.

The principle is never new, for principles are eternal and universal; but the knowledge that the same principle will produce new results when working under new conditions is the key to the unfoldment of infinite possibilities. What we have therefore to consider is the working of Intelligence in providing specific conditions for the operation of universal principles, so as to bring about new results which will transcend our past experiences. The process does not consist in the introduction of new elements, but in making new combinations of elements which are always present; just as our ancestors had no conception of carriages that could go without horses, and yet by a suitable combination of elements which were always in existence, such vehicles are common objects in our streets today. How, then, is the power of Intelligence to be brought to bear upon the generic law of the relation between the Individual and the Universal so as to specialize it into the production of greater results than those which we have hitherto obtained?

All the practical attainments of science, which place the civilized world of today in advance of the times of King Alfred or Charlemagne, have been gained by a uniform method, and that a very simple one. It is by always enquiring what is the affirmative factor in any existing combination, and asking ourselves why, in that particular combination, it does not act beyond certain limits. What makes the thing a success, so far as it goes, and what prevents it going further? Then, by carefully considering the nature of the affirmative factor, we see what sort of conditions to provide to enable it to express itself more fully. This is the scientific method; it has proved itself true in respect of material things, and there is no reason why it should not be equally reliable in respect of spiritual things also.

Taking this as our method, we ask, What is the affirmative factor in the whole creation, and in ourselves as included in the creation, and, as we found in the first lecture, this factor is Spirit—that invisible power which concentrates the primordial ether into forms, and endows those forms with various modes of motion, from the simply mechanical motion of the planet up to the volitional motion in man. And, since this is so, the primary affirmative factor can only be the Feeling and the Thought of the Universal Spirit.* Now, by the hypothesis of the case, the Universal Spirit must be the Pure Essence of Life, and therefore its feeling and thought can only be towards the continually increasing expression of the livingness which it is; and accordingly the specialization, of which we are in search, must be along the line of affording it a centre from which it may more perfectly realize this feeling and express this thought; in other words the way to specialize the generic principle of Spirit is by providing new mental conditions in consonance with its own original nature.

The scientific method of enquiry therefore brings us to the conclusion that the required conditions for translating the racial or generic operation of the Spirit into a specialized individual operation is a new way of *thinking*—a mode of thought concurring with, and not in opposition to, the essential forward movement of the Creative Spirit itself. This implies an entire

*See my *Edinburgh Lectures on Mental Science*.

reversal of our old conceptions. Hitherto we have taken forms and conditions as the starting point of our thought and inferred that *they* are the causes of mental states; now we have learnt that the true order of the creative process is exactly the reverse, and that thought and feeling are the causes, and forms and conditions the effects. When we have learnt this lesson we have grasped the foundation principle on which individual specialization of the generic law of the creative process becomes a practical possibility.

New Thought, then, is not the name of a particular sect, but is the essential factor by which our own future development is to be carried on; and its essence consists in seeing the relation of things in a New Order. Hitherto we have inverted the true order of cause and effect; now, by carefully considering the real nature of the Principle of Causation in itself—*causa causans* as distinguished from *causa causata*—we return to the true order and adopt a new method of thinking in accordance with it.

In themselves this order and this method of thinking are not new. They are older than the foundation of the world, for they are those of the Creative Spirit itself; and all through the ages this teaching has been handed down under various forms, the true meaning of which has been perceived only by a few in each generation. But as the light breaks in upon any individual it is a new light to him, and so to each one in succession it becomes the New Thought. And when anyone reaches it, he finds himself in a New Order. He continues indeed to be included in the universal order of the cosmos, but in a perfectly different way to what he had previously supposed; for, from his new standpoint, he finds that he is included, not so much as a part of the general effect, but as a part of the general cause; and when he perceives this he then sees that the method of his further advance must be by letting the General Cause flow more and more freely into his own specific centre, and he therefore seeks to provide thought conditions which will enable him to do so.

Then, still employing the scientific method of following up the affirmative factor, he realizes that this universal causative power, by whatever name he may call it, manifests as Supreme Intelligence in the adaptation of means to ends. It does so in the mechanism of the planet, in the production of supply for the support of physical life, and in the maintenance of the race as a whole. True, the investigator is met at every turn with individual failure; but his answer to this is that there is no cosmic failure, and that the apparent individual failure is itself a part of the cosmic process, and will diminish in proportion as the individual attains to the recognition of the Moving Principle of that process, and provides the necessary conditions to enable it to take a new starting point in his own individuality. Now, one of these conditions is to recognize it as Intelligence, and to remember that when working through our own mentality it in no way changes its essential nature, just as electricity loses none of its essential qualities in passing through the special apparatus which enables it to manifest as light.

When we see this, our line of thought will run something as follows: "My mind is a centre of Divine operation. The Divine operation is always for expansion and fuller expression, and this means the production of something beyond what has gone before, something entirely new, not included in past experience, though proceeding out of it by an orderly sequence of growth. Therefore, since the Divine cannot change its inherent nature, it must operate in the same manner in me; consequently in my own special world, of which I am the centre, it will move forward to produce new conditions, always in advance of any that have gone before." This is a legitimate line of argument, from the premises established in the recognition of the relation between the individual and the Universal Mind; and it results in our looking to the Divine Mind, not only as creative, but also as directive—that is as determining the actual forms which the conditions for its manifestation will take in our own particular world, as well as supplying the energy for their production. We miss the point of the relation between the individual and the universal, if we do not see that the Originating Spirit is a *forming* power. It is the forming power throughout nature, and if we would specialize it we must learn to trust its formative quality when operating from its new starting point in ourselves.

But the question naturally arises, If this is so, what part is taken by the individual? Our part is to provide a concrete centre round which the Divine energies can play. In the generic order of being we exercise upon it a force of attraction in accordance with the innate pattern of our particular individuality; and as we begin to realize the Law of this relation, we, in our turn, are attracted towards the Divine along the lines of least resistance, that is on those lines which are most natural to our special bent of mind. In this way we throw out certain aspirations with the result that we intensify our attraction of the Divine forces in a certain specific manner, and they then begin to act both through us and around us in accordance with our aspirations. This is the rationale of the reciprocal action between the Universal Mind and the individual mind, and this shows us that our desires should not be directed so much to the acquisition of particular *things* as to the reproduction in ourselves of particular phases of the Spirit's activity; and this, being in its very nature creative, is bound to externalize as corresponding things and circumstances. Then, when these external facts appear in the circle of our objective life, we must work upon them from the objective standpoint. This is where many fall short of completed work. They realize the subjective or creative process, but do not see that it must be followed by an objective or constructive process, and consequently they are unpractical dreamers and never reach the stage of completed work. The creative process brings the materials and conditions for the work to our hands; then we must make use of them with diligence and common sense—God will provide the food, but He will not cook the dinner.

This, then, is the part taken by the individual, and it is thus that he becomes a distributing centre of the Divine energy, neither on the one hand trying to lead it like a blind force, nor on the other being himself under a blind unreasoning impulsion from it. He receives guidance because he seeks guidance; and he both seeks and receives acording to a Law which he is able to recognize; so that he no more sacrifices his liberty or dwarfs his powers than does an engineer who submits to the generic laws of electricity, in order to apply them to some specific purpose. The more intimate his knowledge of this Law of Reciprocity becomes, the more he finds that it leads on to Liberty, on the same principle by which we find in physical science that nature obeys us precisely in the same degree to which we first obey nature. As the esoteric maxim has it "What is a truth on one plane is a truth on all." But the key to this enfranchisement of body, mind, and circumstances is in that new thought which becomes creative of new conditions, because it realizes the true order of the creative process. Therefore it is that, if we would bring a new order of Life, Light, and Liberty into our lives we must commence by bringing a new order into our thought, and find in ourselves the starting point of a new creative series, not by the force of personal will, but by union with the Divine Spirit, which in the expression of its inherent Love and Beauty, makes all things new.

4

THE LIFE OF THE SPIRIT

THE THREE preceding lectures have touched upon certain fundamental truths in a definite order—first the nature of the Originating Spirit itself, next the generic relation of the individual to this All-embracing Spirit, and lastly the way to specialize this relation so as to obtain greater results from it than spontaneously arise by its merely generic action, and we have found that this can only be done through a new order of thought. This sequence is logical because it implies a Power, an Individual who understands the Power, and a Method of applying the power deduced from understanding its nature. These are general principles without realizing which it is impossible to proceed further, but assuming that the reader has grasped their significance, we may now go on to consider their application in greater detail.

Now this application must be a personal one, for it is only through the individual that the higher specialization of the power can take place, but at the same time this must not lead us to suppose that the individual, himself, brings the creative force into being. To suppose this is inversion; and we cannot impress upon ourselves too deeply that the relation of the individual to the Divine Spirit is that of a distributor, and not that of the original creator. If this is steadily borne in mind the way will become clear, otherwise we shall be led into confusion.

What, then, is the Power which we are to distribute? It is the Originating Spirit itself. We are sure that it is this because the new order of thought always begins at the beginning of any series which it contemplates bringing into manifestation, and it is based upon the fact that the origin of everything is Spirit. It is in this that its creative power resides; hence the person who is in the true new order of thought assumes as an axiomatic fact that what he has to distribute, or differentiate into manifestation, is nothing else than the Originating Spirit. This being the case, it is evident that the *purpose* of the distribution must be the more perfect expression of the Originating Spirit as that which it is in itself, and what it is in itself is emphatically Life. What is seeking for expression, then, is the perfect Livingness of the Spirit; and this expression is to be found, through ourselves, by means of our renewed mode of thought. Let us see, then, how our new order of thought, with regard to the Principle of Life, is likely to operate. In our old order of thought we have always associated Life with the physical body—life has been for us the supreme physical fact. Now, however, we know that Life is much more than this; but, as the greater includes the less, it includes physical life as one mode of its manifestation. The true order does not require us to deny the reality of physical life or to call it an illusion; on the contrary it sees in physical life the completion of a great creative series, but it assigns it the proper place in that series, which is what the old mode of thought did not.

When we realize the truth about the Creative Process, we see that the originating life is not physical; its livingness consists in thought and feeling. By this inner movement it throws out vehicles through which to function, and these become living forms because of the inner principle which is sustaining them; so that the Life with which we are primarily concerned in the new order is the life of thought and feeling in ourselves as the vehicle, or distributing medium, of the Life of the Spirit.

Then, if we have grasped the idea of the Spirit as the great *forming* Power, as stated in the last lecture, we shall seek in it the fountain-head of Form as well as of Power; and as a logical deduction from this we shall look to it to give form to our thoughts and feelings. If the principle is once recognised the sequence is obvious. The form taken by our outward conditions, whether of body or circumstance, depends on the form taken by our thoughts and feelings, and our thoughts and feelings will take form from that source from which we allow them to receive suggestion. Accordingly if we allow them to accept their fundamental suggestions from the relative and limited, they will assume a corresponding form and transmit them to our external environment, thus repeating the old order of limitation in a ceaselessly recurring round. Now our object is to get out of this circle of limitation, and the only way to do so is to get our thoughts and feelings moulded into new forms continually advancing to greater and greater perfection. To meet this requirement, therefore, there must be a forming power greater than that of our own unaided conceptions, and this is to be found in our realization of the Spirit as the Supreme Beauty, or Wisdom, moulding our thoughts and feelings into shapes harmoniously adjusted to the fullest expression, in and through us, of the Livingness which Spirit is in itself.

Now this is nothing more than transferring to the innermost plane of origination a principle with which all readers who are "in the thought" may be presumed to be quite familiar—the principle of Receptiveness. We all know what is meant by a receptive mental attitude when applied to healing or telepathy; and does it not logically follow that the same principle may be applied to the receiving of life itself from the Supreme Source? What is wanted, therefore, is to place ourselves in a receptive mental attitude towards the Universal Spirit with the intention of receiving its forming influence into our mental substance. It is always the presence of a definite intention that distinguishes the intelligent receptive attitude of mind from a merely sponge-like absorbency, which sucks in any and every influence that may happen to be floating round; for we must not shut our eyes to the fact that there are various influences in the mental atmosphere by which we are surrounded, and some of them of the most undesirable kind. Clear and definite intention is therefore as necessary in our receptive attitude as in our active and creative one; and if our intention is to have our own thoughts and feelings moulded into such forms as to express those of the Spirit, then we establish that relation to the Spirit which, by the conditions of the case, must necessarily lead us to the conception of new ideals vitalised by a power which will enable us to bring them into concrete manifestation. It is in this way that we become differentiating centres of the Divine Thought, giving it expression in form in the world of space and time, and thus is solved the great problem of enabling the Universal to act upon the plane of the particular without being hampered by those limitations which the merely generic law of manifestation imposes upon it. It is just here that subconscious mind performs the function of a "bridge" between the finite and the infinite as noted in my *Edinburgh Lectures on Mental Science* (page 29), and it is for this reason that a recognition of its susceptibility to impression is so important.

By establishing, then, a personal relation to the life of the Spirit, the sphere of the individual becomes enlarged. The reason is that he allows a greater intelligence than his own to take the initiative; and since he knows that this Intelligence is also the very Principle of Life itself, he cannot have any fear that it will act in any way to the diminution of his individual life, for that would be to stultify its own operation—it would be self-destructive action which is a contradiction in terms to the conception of Creative Spirit. Knowing, then, that by its inherent nature this Intelligence can only work to the expansion of the individual life, we can rest upon it with the utmost confidence and trust it to take an initiative which will lead to far greater results than any we could forecast from the standpoint of our own knowledge. So long as we insist on dictating the particular form which the action of the Spirit is to take, we limit it, and so close against ourselves avenues of expansion which might otherwise have been open to us; and if we ask ourselves why we do this we shall find that in the last resort it is because we do not believe in the Spirit as a *forming* power. We have, indeed, advanced to the conception of it as executive power, which will work to a prescribed pattern, but we have yet to grasp the conception of it as versed in the art of design, and capable of elaborating schemes of construction, which will not only be complete in themselves, but also in perfect harmony with one another. When we advance to the conception of the Spirit as containing in itself the ideal of Form as well as of Power, we shall cease from the effort of trying to force things into a particular shape, whether on the inner or the outer plane, and shall be content to trust the inherent harmoniousness or Beauty of the Spirit to produce combinations far in advance of anything that we could have conceived ourselves. This does not mean that we shall reduce ourselves to a condition of apathy, in which all desire, expectation and enthusiasm have been quenched, for these are the mainspring of our mental machinery; but on the contrary their action will be quickened by the knowledge that there is working at the back of them a Formative Principle so infallible that it cannot miss its mark; so that however good and beautiful the existing forms may be, we may always rest in the happy expectation of something still better to come. And it will come by a natural law of growth, because the Spirit is in itself the Principle of Increase. They will grow out of present conditions for the simple reason that if you are to reach some further point it can only be by starting from where you are now. Therefore it is written, "Despise not the day of small things." There is only one proviso attached to this forward movement of the Spirit in the world of our own surroundings, and that is that we shall cooperate with it; and this cooperation consists in making the best use of existing conditions in cheerful reliance on the Spirit of Increase to express itself through us, and for us, because we are in harmony with it. This mental attitude will be found of immense value in setting us free from worry and anxiety, and as a consequence our work will be done in a much more efficient manner. We shall do the present work *for its own sake*, knowing that herein is the principle of unfoldment; and doing it simply for its own sake we shall bring to bear upon it a power of concentration which cannot fail of good results—and this quite naturally and without any toilsome effort. We shall then find that the secret of cooperation is to have faith in ourselves because we first have faith in God; and we shall discover that this Divine self-confidence is something very different from a boastful egotism which assumes a personal superiority over others. It is simply the assurance of a man who knows that he is working in accordance with a law of nature. He does not claim as a personal achievement what the Law does *for* him; but on the other hand he does not trouble himself about outcries against his presumptuous audacity raised by persons who are ignorant of the Law which he is employing. He is therefore neither boastful nor timorous, but simply works on in cheerful expectancy because he knows that his reliance is upon a Law which cannot be broken.

In this way, then, we must realize the Life of the Spirit as being also the Law of the Spirit. The two are identical, and cannot deny themselves. Our recognition of them gives them a new starting point through our own mentality, but they still continue to be the same in their nature, and unless limited or inverted by our mental affirmation of limited or inverted conditions, they are bound to work out into fuller and continually fuller expression of the Life, Love, and Beauty which the Spirit is in itself. Our path, therefore, is plain; it is simply to contemplate the Life, Love, and Beauty of the Originating Spirit and affirm that we are already giving expression to it in our thoughts and in our actions however insignificant they may at present appear. This path may be very narrow and humble in its beginning, but it ever grows wider and mounts higher, for it is the continually expanding expression of the Life of the Spirit which is infinite and knows no limits.

5

ALPHA AND OMEGA

Alpha and Omega, the First and the Last. What does this mean? It means the entire series of causation from the first originating movement to the final and completed result. We may take this on any scale from the creation of a cosmos to the creation of a lady's robe. Everything has its origin in an idea, a thought; and it has its completion in the manifestation of that thought in form. Many intermediate stages are necessary, but the Alpha and Omega of the series are the thought and the thing. This shows us that in essence the thing already existed in the thought. Omega is already potential in Alpha, just as in the Pythagorean system all numbers are said to proceed from unity and to be resolvable back again into it. Now it is this general principle of the already existence of the thing in the thought that we have to lay hold of, and as we find it true in an architect's design of the house that is to be, so we find it true in the great work of the Architect of the Universe. When we see this we have realized a general principle, which we find at work everywhere. That is the meaning of a *general* principle: it can be applied to any sort of subject; and the use of studying general principles is to give them particular application to anything we may have to deal with. Now what we have to deal with most of all is ourselves, and so we come to the consideration of Alpha and Omega in the human being. In the vision of St. John, the speaker of the words, "I am Alpha and Omega, the First and the Last," is described as "Like unto a son of man"—that is, however transcendent the appearance in the vision, it is essentially human, and thus suggests to us the presence of the universal principle at the human level. But the figure in the apocalyptic vision is not that of man as we ordinarily know him. It is that of Omega as it subsists enshrined in Alpha; it is the ideal of humanity as it subsists in the Divine Mind which was manifested in objective form to the eyes of the seer, and therefore presented the Alpha and Omega of that idea in all the majesty of Divine glory.

But if we grasp the truth that the thing is already existent in the thought, do we not see that this transcendent Omega must be already existent in the Divine ideal of every one of us? If on the plane of the absolute time is not, then does it not follow that this glorified humanity is a present fact in the Divine Mind? And if this is so, then this fact is eternally true regarding every human being. But if it is true that the thing exists in the thought, it is equally true that the thought finds form in the thing; and since things exist under the relative conditions of time and space, they are necessarily subject to a law of Growth, so that while the subsistence of the thing in the thought is perfect *ab initio*, the expression of the thought in the thing is a matter of gradual development. This is a point which we must never lose sight of in our studies; and we must never lose sight of the perfection of the thing in the thought because we do not yet see the perfection of the thought in the thing. Therefore we must remember that man, as we know him now, has by no means reached the ultimate of his evolution. We are only yet in the making, but we have now reached a point where we can facilitate the evolutionary process by conscious cooperation with the Creative Spirit. Our share in this work commences with the recognition of the Divine ideal of man, and thus finding the pattern by which we are to be guided. For since the person to be created after this pattern is ourself, it follows that, by whatever processes the Divine ideal transforms itself into concrete reality, the place where those processes are to work must be within ourselves; in other words, the creative action of the Spirit takes place through the laws of our own mentality. If it is a true maxim that the thing must take form in the thought before the thought can take form in the thing, then it is plain that the Divine Ideal can only be externalized in our objective life in proportion as it is first formed in our thought; and it takes form in our thought only to the extent to which we apprehend its existence in the Divine Mind. By the nature of the relation between the individual mind and the Universal Mind it is strictly a case of reflection; and in proportion as the mirror of our own mind blurs or clearly reflects the image of the Divine ideal, so will it give rise to a correspondingly feeble or vigorous reproduction of it in our external life.

This being the rationale of the matter, why should we limit our conception of the Divine ideal of ourselves? Why should we say, "I am too mean a creature ever to reflect so glorious an image"—or "God never intended such a limitless ideal to be reproduced in human beings." In saying such things we expose our ignorance of the whole Law of the Creative Process. We shut our eyes to the fact that the Omega of completion already subsists in the Alpha of conception, and that the Alpha of conception would be nothing but a lying illusion if it was not capable of expression in the Omega of completion. The creative process in us is that we become the individual reflection of what we realize God to be relatively to ourselves, and therefore if we realize the Divine Spirit as the *infinite potential* of all that can constitute a perfected human being, this conception must, by the Law of the Creative Process, gradually build up a corresponding image in our mind, which in turn will act upon our external conditions.

This, by the laws of mind, is the nature of the process and it shows us what St. Paul means when he speaks of Christ being formed in us (Gal. 4:19) and what in another place he calls being renewed in knowledge after the image of Him that created us (Col. 3:10). It is a thoroughly logical sequence of cause and effect, and what we require is to see more clearly the Law of this sequence and use it intelligently—that is why St. Paul says it is being "renewed in knowledge": it is a New Knowledge, the recognition of principles which we had not previously apprehended. Now the fact which, in our past experience, we have not grasped is that the human mind forms a new point of departure for the work of the Creative Spirit; and in proportion as we see this more and more clearly, the more we shall find ourselves entering into a new order of life in which we become less and less subject to the old limitations. This is not a reward arbitrarily bestowed upon us for holding dogmatically to certain mere verbal statements, but it is the natural result of understanding the supreme law of our own being. On its own plane it is as purely scientific as the law of chemical reaction; only here we are not dealing with the interaction of secondary causes but with the Self-originating action of Spirit. Hence a new force has to be taken into account which does not occur in physical science, the power of Feeling. Thought creates form, but it is feeling that gives vitality to thought. Thought without feeling may be constructive as in some great engineering work, but it can never be creative as in the work of the artist or musician; and that which originates within itself a new order of causation is, so far as all pre-existing forms are concerned, a creation *ex nihilo*, and is therefore Thought expressive of Feeling. It is this indissoluble union of Thought and Feeling that distinguishes creative thought from merely analytical thought and places it in a different category; and therefore if we are to afford a new starting point for carrying on the work of creation it must be by assimilating the feeling of the Originating Spirit as part and parcel of its thought—it is that entering into the Mind of the Spirit of which I spoke in the first address.

Now the images in the Mind of the Spirit must necessarily be *generic*. The reason for this is that by its very nature the Principle of Life must be prolific, that is, tending to Multiplicity, and therefore the original Thought-image must be fundamental to whole races, and not exclusive to particular individuals. Consequently the images in the Mind of the Spirit must be absolute types of the true essentials of the perfect development of the race, just what Plato meant by archetypal ideas. This is the perfect subsistence of the thing in the thought. Therefore it is that our evolution as centres of *creative* activity, the exponents of new laws, and through them of new conditions, depends on our realizing in the Divine Mind the archetype of mental perfection, at once as thought and feeling. But when we find all this in the Divine Mind, do we not meet with an infinite and glorious Personality? There is nothing lacking of all that we can understand by Personality, excepting outward form; and since the very essence of telepathy is that it dispenses with the physical presence, we find ourselves in a position of interior communion with a Personality at once Divine and Human. This is that Personality of the Spirit which St. John saw in the apocalyptic vision, and which by the very conditions of the case is the Alpha and Omega of Humanity.

But, as I have said, it is simply *generic* in itself, and it becomes active and specific only by a purely personal relation to the individual. But once more we must realize that nothing can take place except according to Law, and therefore this specific relation is nothing arbitrary, but arises out of the generic Law applied under specific conditions. And since what makes a law generic is precisely the fact that it does not supply the specific conditions, it follows that the conditions for the specialising of the Law must be provided by the individual. Then it is that his recognition of the originating creative movement, as arising from combined Thought and Feeling, becomes a practical working asset. He realizes that there is a Heart and Mind of the Spirit reciprocal to his own heart and mind, that he is not dealing with a filmy abstraction, nor yet with a mere mathematical sequence, but with something that is pulsating with a Life as warm and vivid and full of interest as his own—nay, more so, for it is the Infinite of all that he himself is. And his recognition goes even further than this, for since this specialization can only take place through the individual himself, it logically follows that the Life, which he thus specializes, become *his own* life. *Quoad* the individual it does not know itself apart from him. But this self-recognition through the individual cannot in any way change the inherent nature of the Creative Spirit, and therefore to the extent to which the individual perceives its identification with himself, he places himself under its guidance, and so he becomes one of those who are "led by the Spirit." Thus he begins to find the Alpha and Omega of the Divine ideal reproduced in himself—in a very small degree at present, but containing the principle of perpetual growth into an infinite expansion of which we can as yet form no conception.

St. John sums up the whole of this position in his memorable words: "Beloved now are we the Sons of God, and it doth not yet appear what we *shall* be; but we know that when He shall appear (*i.e.*, become clear to us) we shall be like Him; for (*i.e.*, the reason of all this) we shall see Him as He is" (1 John 3:2).

6

THE CREATIVE POWER OF THOUGHT

ONE OF THE GREAT axioms in the new order of ideas, of which I have spoken, is that our Thought possesses creative power, and since the whole superstructure depends on this foundation, it is well to examine it carefully. Now the starting point is to see that Thought, or purely mental action, is the only possible source from which the existing creation could ever have come into manifestation at all, and it is on this account that in the preceding addresses I have laid stress on the origin of the cosmos. It is therefore not necessary to go over this ground again, and we will start this morning's enquiry on the assumption that every manifestation is in essence the expression of a Divine Thought. This being so, our own mind is the expression of a Divine Thought. The Divine Thought has produced something which itself is capable of thinking; but the question is whether its thinking has the same creative quality as that of the Parent Mind.

Now by the very hypothesis of the case the whole Creative Process consists in the continual pressing forward of the Universal Spirit for expression through the individual and particular, and Spirit in its different modes is therefore the Life and Substance of the universe. Hence it follows that if there is to be an expression of thinking power it can only be by expressing the same thinking power which subsists latent in the Originating Spirit. If it were less than this it would only be some sort of mechanism and would not be thinking power, so that to be thinking power at all it must be identical in kind with that of the Originating Spirit. It is for this reason that man is said to be created in the image and likeness of God; and if we realize that it is impossible for him to be otherwise, we shall find a firm foundation from which to draw many important deductions.

But if our thought possesses this creative power, why are we hampered by adverse conditions? The answer is, because hitherto we have used our power invertedly. We have taken the starting point of our thought from external facts and consequently created a repetition of facts of a similar nature, and so long as we do this we must needs go on perpetuating the old circle of limitation. And, owing to the sensitiveness of the subconscious mind to suggestion (see *Edinburgh Lectures*, chapter 5) we are subject to a very powerful negative influence from those who are unacquainted with affirmative principles, and thus race-beliefs and the thought-currents of our more immediate environment tend to consolidate our own inverted thinking. It is therefore not surprising that the creative power of our thought, thus used in a wrong direction, has produced the limitations of which we complain. The remedy, then, is by reversing our method of thinking, and instead of taking external facts as our starting point, taking the inherent nature of mental power as our starting point. We have already gained two great steps in this direction, first by seeing that the whole manifested cosmos could have had its origin nowhere but in mental power, and secondly by realizing that our own mental power must be the same in kind with that of the Originating Mind.

Now we can go a step further and see how this power in ourselves can be perpetuated and intensified. By the nature of the creative process your mind is itself a thought of the Parent Mind; so, as long as this thought of the Universal Mind subsists, *you* will subsist, for you *are* it. But so long as you think this thought it continues to subsist, and necessarily remains present in the Divine Mind, thus fulfilling the logical conditions required for the perpetuation of the individual life. A poor analogy of the process may be found in a self-influencing dynamo where the magnetism generates the current and the current intensifies the magnetism with the result of producing a still stronger current until the limit of saturation is reached; only in the substantive infinitude of the Universal Mind and the potential infinitude of the Individual Mind there is no limit of saturation. Or we may compare the interaction of the two minds to two mirrors, a great and a small one, opposite each other, with the word "Life" engraved on the large one. Then, by the law of reflection, the word "Life" will also appear on the image of the smaller mirror reflected in the greater. Of course these are only very imperfect analogies; but if you can once grasp the idea of your own individuality as a thought in the Divine Mind which is able to perpetuate itself by thinking of itself as the thought which it is, you have got at the root of the whole matter, and by the same process you will not only perpetuate your life but will also expand it.

When we realize this on the one hand, and on the other that all external conditions, including the body, are produced by thought, we find ourselves standing between two infinites, the infinite of Mind and the infinite of Substance—from both of which we can draw what we will, and mould specific conditions out of the Universal Substance by the Creative Power which we draw in from the Universal Mind. But we must recollect that this is not by the force of personal will upon the substance, which is an error that will land us in all sorts of inversion, but by realizing our mind as a channel through which the Universal Mind operates upon substances in a particular way, according to the mode of thought which we are seeking to embody. If, then, our thought is habitually concentrated upon principles rather than on particular things, realizing that principles are nothing else than the Divine Mind in operation, we shall find that they will necessarily germinate to produce their own expression in corresponding facts, thus verifying the words of the Great Teacher, "Seek ye first the Kingdom of God and His righteousness and all these things shall be added unto you."

But we must never lose sight of the reason for the creative power of our thought, that it is because our mind is itself a thought of the Divine Mind, and that consequently our increase in livingness and creative power must be in exact proportion to our perception of our relation to the Parent Mind. In such considerations as these is to be found the philosophical basis of the Bible doctrine of "Sonship," with its culmination in the conception of the Christ. These are not mere fancies but the expression of strictly scientific principles, in their application to the deepest problems of the individual life; and their basis is that each one's world, whether in or out of the flesh, must necessarily be created by his own consciousness, and, in its turn, his mode of consciousness will necessarily take its colour from his conception of his relation to the Divine Mind—to the exclusion of light and colour, if he realizes no Divine Mind, and to their building up into forms of beauty in proportion as he realizes his identity of being with that All- originating Spirit which is Light, Love, and Beauty in itself. Thus the great creative work of Thought in each of us is to make us consciously "sons and daughters of the Almighty," realizing that by our divine origin we can never be really separated from the Parent Mind which is continually seeking expression through us, and that any apparent separation is due to our own misconception of the true nature of the inherent relation between the Universal and the Individual. This is the lesson which the Great Teacher has so luminously put before us in the parable of the Prodigal Son.

7

THE GREAT AFFIRMATIVE

THE GREAT AFFIRMATIVE appears in two modes, the cosmic and the individual. In its essence it is the same in both, but in each it works from a different standpoint. It is always the principle of Being—that which *is*, as distinguished from that which is not; but to grasp the true significance of this saying we must understand what is meant by "that which is not." It is something more than mere non-existence, for obviously we should not trouble ourselves about what is non-existent. It is that which both is and is not at the same time, and the thing that answers to this description is "Conditions." The little affirmative is that which affirms particular conditions as all that it can grasp, while the great affirmative grasps a wider conception, the conception of that which gives rise to conditions. Cosmically it is that power of Spirit which sends forth the whole creation as its expression of itself, and it is for this reason that I have drawn attention in the preceding lectures to the idea of the creation *ex nihilo* of the whole visible universe. As Eastern and Western Scriptures alike tell us it is the breathing-forth of Original Spirit; and if you have followed what I have said regarding the reproduction of this Spirit in the individual—that by the very nature of the creative process the human mind must be of the same quality with the Divine Mind—then we find that a second mode of the Originating Spirit becomes possible, namely that of operation through the individual mind. But whether acting cosmically or personally it is always the same Spirit and therefore cannot lose its inherent character which is that of the Power which creates *ex nihilo*. It is the direct contradiction of the maxim "ex nihilo nihil fit"—nothing can be made out of nothing; and it is the recognition of the presence in ourselves of this power, which can make something out of nothing, that is the key to our further progress. As the logical outcome of the cosmic creative process, the evolutionary work reaches a point where the Originating Power creates an image of itself; and thus affords a fresh point of departure from which it can work specifically, just as in the cosmic process it works generically. From this new standpoint it does not in any way contradict the laws of the cosmic order, but proceeds to specialize them, and thus to bring out results through the individual which could not be otherwise attained.

Now the Spirit does this by the same method as in the Original Creation, namely by creating *ex nihilo*; for otherwise it would be bound by the limitations necessarily inherent in the cosmic *form* of things, and so no fresh creative starting point would have been attained. This is why the Bible lays such stress on the principle of Monogenesis, or creation from a single power instead of from a pair or syzegy; and it is on this account that we are told that this One-ness of God is the foundation of all the commandments, and that the "Son of God" is declared to be "monogenes" or one-begotten, for that is the correct translation of the Greek word. The immense importance of this principle of creation from a single power will become apparent as we realize more fully the results proceeding from the assumption of the opposite principle, or the dualism of the creative power; but as the discussion of this great subject would require a volume to itself, I must, at present, content myself with saying that this insistence of the Bible upon the singleness of the Creative Power is based upon a knowledge which goes to the very root of esoteric principles, and is therefore not to be set aside in favour of dualistic systems, though superficially the latter may appear more consonant to reason.

If, then, it is possible to put the Great Affirmation into words it is that God is ONE and that this ONE finds centre in ourselves; and if the full meaning of this statement is realized, the logical result will be found to be a new creation both in and from ourselves. We shall realize in ourselves the working of a new principle whose distinguishing feature is its simplicity. It is ONE-ness and is not troubled about any second. Hence what it contemplates is not how its action will be modified by that of some second principle, something which will compel it to work in a particular manner and so limit it; but what it contemplates is its own Unity. Then it perceives that its Unity consists in a greater and a lesser movement, just as the rotation of the earth on its axis does not interfere with its rotation around the sun but are both motions of the same unit, and are definitely related to each other. In like manner we find that the Spirit is moving simultaneously in the macrocosm of the universe and in the microcosm of the individual, and the two movements harmonize because they are that of the same Spirit, and the latter is included in the former and presupposes it. The Great Affirmation, therefore, is the perception that the "I AM" is ONE, always harmonious with itself, and including all things in this harmony for the simple reason that there is no second creative power; and when the individual realizes that this always-single power is the root of his own being, and therefore has centre in himself and finds expression through him, he learns to trust its singleness and the consequent harmony of its action *in* him with what it is doing *around* him. Then he sees that the affirmation "I and my Father are ONE" is a necessary deduction from a correct apprehension of the fundamental principles of being; and then, on the principle that the less must be included in the greater, he desires that harmonious unity of action be maintained by the adaptation of his own particular movement to the larger movement of the Spirit working as the Creative Principle through the great whole. In this way we become centres through which the creative forces find specialization by the development of that personal factor on which the specific application of general laws must always depend. A specific sort of individuality is formed, capable of being the link between the great Spiritual Power of the universal and the manifestation of the relative in time and space because it consciously partakes of both; and because the individual of this class recognizes the singleness of the Spirit as the starting point of all things, he endeavours to withdraw his mind from all arguments derived from external conditions, whether past or present, and to fix it upon the forward movement of the Spirit which he knows to be always identical both in the universe and in himself. He ceases the attempt to dictate to the Spirit, because he does not see in it a mere blind force, but reveres it as the Supreme Intelligence; and on the other hand he does not grovel before it in doubt and fear, because he knows it is one with himself and is realizing itself through him, and therefore cannot have any purpose antagonistic to his own individual welfare. Realizing this, he deliberately places his thoughts under the guidance of the Divine Spirit, knowing that his outward acts and conditions must thereby be brought into harmony with the great forward movement of the Spirit, not only at the stage he has now reached, but at all future stages. He does not at all deny the power of his own thought as the creative agent in his own personal world—on the contrary it is precisely on the knowledge of this fact that his perception of the true adjustment between the principles of Life is based; but for this very reason he is the more solicitous to be led by that Wisdom which can see what he cannot see, so that his personal control over the conditions of his own life may be employed to its continual increase and development.

In this way our affirmation of the "I am" ceases to be the petulant assertion of our limited personality and becomes the affirmation that the Great I AM affirms its own I AM-ness both in us and through us, and thus our use of the words becomes in very truth the Great Affirmative, or that which is the root of all being as distinguished from that which has no being in itself but is merely externalized by being as the vehicle for its expression. We shall realize our true place as subordinate creative centres, perfectly independent of existing conditions because the creative process is that of monogenesis and requires no other factor than the Spirit for its exercise, but at the same time subordinate to the Divine Spirit in the greatness of its inherent forward movement because there is only ONE Spirit and it cannot from one centre antagonize what it is doing from another. Thus the Great Affirmation makes us children of the Great King, at once living in obedience to that Power which is above us, and exercising this same power over all that world of secondary causation which is below us.

Thus in our measure and station each one of us will receive the mission of the I AM.

8

CHRIST THE FULFILLING OF THE LAW

Think not that I am come to destroy the law or the prophets: I am not come to destroy but to fulfil. (Matt. 5:17)

Christ is the end of the law for righteousness to everyone that believeth. (Rom. 10:4)

IF THESE WORDS are the utterance of a mere sectarian superstition they are worthless; but if they are the statement of a great principle, then it is worth our while to enquire what that principle is. The fulfilling of anything is the bringing into complete realization of all that it potentially contains, and so the filling of any law to its fulness means bringing out all the possibilities which are hidden in it. This is precisely the method which has brought forth all the advances of material civilization. The laws of nature are the same now that they were in the days of our rugged Anglo-Saxon ancestors, but they brought out only an infinitesimal fraction of the possibilities which those laws contain; now we have brought out a good deal more, but we have by no means exhausted them, and so we continue to advance, not by contradicting natural laws, but by more fully realizing their capacity. Why should we not, then, apply the same method to ourselves and see whether there are no potentialities hidden away in the law of our own being which we have not as yet by any means brought to their fulfilment? We talk of a good time coming and of the ameliorating of the race; but do we reflect that the race is composed of individuals and that therefore real advance is to be made only by individual improvement, and not by Act of Parliament? and if so, then the individual with whom to begin is ourself.

The complete manifestation of the Law of Individuality is the end or purpose of the Bible teaching concerning Christ. It is a teaching based upon Law, spiritual and mental, fully recognizing that no effect can be produced except by the operation of an adequate cause; and Christ is set before us both as explaining the causes and exhibiting the full measure of the effects. All this is according to Law; and the importance of its being according to Law is that Law is universal, and the potentialities of the Law are therefore inherent in everyone—there is no special law for anybody, but anybody can specialize the law by using it with a fuller understanding of how much can be got out of it; and the purpose of the Scripture teaching regarding Christ is to help us to do this.

The preceding lectures have led us step by step to see that the Originating Spirit, which first brought the world into existence, is also the root of our own individuality, and is therefore always ready, by its inherent nature, to continue the creative process from this individual standpoint as soon as the necessary conditions are provided, and these conditions are thought-conditions. Then by realizing the relation of Christ to the Originating Mind, the Parent Spirit or "Father," we receive a *standard* of thought which is bound to act creatively bringing out all the potentialities of our hidden being. Now the relation of Christ to the "Father" is that of the Archetypal Idea in the All-creating Mind of which I have previously spoken, and so we arrive at the conception of the Christ-idea as a universal principle, and as being an idea therefore capable of reproduction in the individual Mind, thus explaining St. Paul's meaning when he speaks of Christ being formed in us. It is here that the principle of monogenesis comes in, that principle which I have endeavoured to describe in the earlier part of the present series as originating the whole manifested creation by an internal action of the Spirit upon itself; and it is the entire absence of control by any second power that renders the realization in external actuality of a purely mental ideal possible. For this reason systematic spiritual study commences with the contemplation of the existing cosmos, and we then transfer the conception of the monogenetic power of the Spirit from the cosmos to the individual and realize that the same Spirit is able to do the same thing in ourselves. This is the New Thought which in time will fulfil itself in the New Order, and we thus provide new thought-conditions which enable the Spirit to carry on its creative work from a new standpoint, that of our own individuality. This attainment by the Spirit of a new starting point is what is meant by the esoteric doctrine of the Octave. The Octave is the starting point of a new series reduplicating the starting point of the previous series at a different level, just as does the octave note in music. We find this principle constantly referred to in

Scripture—the completion of a prior series in the number Seven, and the starting of a new series by the number Eight, which takes the same place in the second series that the number One did in the first. The second series comes out of the first by natural growth and could not come into existence without it, hence the First or Originating number of the second series is the Eighth if we regard the second series as the prolongation of the first. Seven is the numerical correspondence of complete manifestation because it is the combination of three and four, which respectively represent the complete working of the spiritual and material factors—involution and evolution—and thus together constitute the finished whole. Students of the Tarot will here realize the process by which the Yod of Yod becomes the Yod of He. It is for this reason that the primary or cosmic creation terminates in the rest of the Seventh Day, for it can proceed no further until a fresh starting point is found. But when this fresh starting point is found in Man realizing his relation to the "Father," we start a new series and strike the Creative Octave and therefore the Resurrection takes place, not on the Sabbath or Seventh Day, but on the Eighth day which then becomes the First day of the new creative week. The *principle* of the Resurrection is the realization by man of his individualization of the Spirit and his recognition of the fact that, since the Spirit is always the same Spirit, it becomes the Alpha of a new creation from his own centre of being.

Now all this is necessarily an interior process taking place on the mental plane; but if we realize that the creative process is always primarily one of involution, or formation in the spiritual world, we shall grasp something of the meaning of Christ as "The Son of God"—the concentration of the Universal Spirit into a Personality on the spiritual plane correlatively to the individuality of each one who affords the necessary thought-conditions. To all who apprehend it there is then discovered in the Universal Spirit the presence of a Divine Individuality reciprocal to that of the individual man, the recognition of which is the practical solution of all metaphysical problems regarding the emanation of the individual soul from the Universal Spirit and the relations arising therefrom; for it takes these matters out of the region of intellectual speculation, which is never creative but only analytical, and transfers them to the region of feeling and spiritual sensation which is the abode of the creative forces. This personal recognition of the Divine then affords us a new basis of Affirmation, and we need no longer trouble to go further back in order to analyze it, because we know experimentally that it is there; so now we find the starting point of the new creation ready-made for us according to the archetypal pattern in the Divine Mind itself and therefore perfectly correctly formed. When once this truth is clearly apprehended, whether we reach it by an intellectual process or by simple intuition, we can make it our starting point and claim to have our thought permeated by the creative power of the Spirit on this basis.

But vast as is the conception thus reached we must remember that it is still a starting point. It, indeed, transcends our previous range of ideas and so presents a culmination of the cosmic creative series which passes beyond that series and thus brings us to number Eight or the Octave; but on this very account it is the number One of a new creative series which is personal to the individual.

Then, because the Spirit is always the same, we may look for a repetition of the creative process at a higher level, and, as we all know, that process consists first of the involution of Spirit into Substance, and consequently of the subsequent evolution of Substance into forms continually increasing in fitness as vehicles for Spirit; so now we may look for a repetition of this universal process from its new starting point in the individual mind and expect a corresponding externalization in accordance with our familiar axiom that thoughts are things.

Now it is as such an external manifestation of the Divine ideal that the Christ of the Gospels is set before us. I do not wish to dogmatize, but I will only say that the more clearly we realize the nature of the creative process on the spiritual side the more the current objections to the Gospel narrative lose their force; and it appears to me that to deny that narrative as a point-blank impossibility is to make a similar affirmation with regard to the power of the Spirit in ourselves. You cannot affirm a principle and deny it in the same breath; and if we affirm the externalizing power of the Spirit in our own case, I do not see how we can logically lay down a limit for its action and say that under highly specialized conditions it could not produce highly specialized effects. It is for this reason that St. John puts the question of Christ manifest in the flesh as the criterion of the whole matter (1 John 4:2). If the Spirit can create at all then you cannot logically limit the extent or method of its working; and since the basis of our expectation of individual expansion is the limitless creative power of the Spirit, to reject the Christ of the Gospels as an impossibility is to cut away the ground from under our own feet. It is one thing to say "I do not understand why the Spirit should have worked in that way"—that is merely an honest statement of our present stage of knowledge, or we may even go the length of saying that we do not feel convinced that it did work in that way—that is a true confession of our intellectual difficultly—but certainly those who are professedly relying on the power of the Spirit to produce external results cannot say that it does not possess that power, or possesses it only in a limited degree; the position is logically self-destructive. What we should do therefore, is to suspend judgment and follow the light as far as we can see it, and bye-and-bye it will become clearer to us. There are, it appears to me, occult heights in the doctrine of Christ designed by the Supreme Wisdom to counteract corresponding occult depths in the Mystery of Darkness. I do not think it is at all necessary, or even possible, for us to scale these heights or fathom those depths, with our present infantile intelligence, but if we realize how completely the law of our being receives its fulfilment in Christ as far as we know that law, may we not well conceive that there are yet deeper phases of that law the existence of which we can only faintly surmise by intuition? Occasionally just the fringe of the veil is lifted for some of us, but that momentary glance is enough to show us that there are powers and mysteries beyond our present conception. But even there Law reigns supreme, and therefore taking Christ as our basis and starting point, we start with the Law already fulfilled, whether in those things which are familiar to us or in those realms which are beyond our thought, and so we need have no fear of evil. Our starting point is that of a divinely ordained security from which we may quietly grow into that higher evolution which is the fulfilment of the law of our own being.

9

THE STORY OF EDEN

THE WHOLE BIBLE and the whole history of the world, past, present and future, are contained in embryo in the story of Eden, for they are nothing else than the continuous unfolding of certain great principles which are there allegorically stated. That this is by no means a new notion is shown by the following quotation from Origen: "Who is there so foolish and without common sense as to believe that God planted trees in the Garden of Eden like a husbandman; and planted therein the tree of life perceptible to the eyes and to the senses, which gave life to the eater; and another tree which gave to the eater a knowledge of good and evil? I believe that everybody must regard these as figures under which a recondite sense is concealed." Let us, then, follow up the suggestion of this early Father of the Church, and enquire what may be the "recondite sense" concealed under this figure of the two trees. On the face of the story there are two roots, one of Life and the other of Death, two fundamental principles bringing about diametrically opposite results. The distinctive mark of the latter is that it is the knowledge of good and evil, that is to say, the recognition of two antagonistic principles, and so requiring a knowledge of the relations between them to enable us to continually make the needful adjustments to keep ourselves going. Now, in appearance this is exceedingly specious. It looks so entirely reasonable that we do not see its ultimate destructiveness; and so we are told that Eve ate the fruit because she "saw that the tree was pleasant to the eyes." But careful consideration will show us in what the destructive nature of this principle consists. It is based on the fallacy that good is limited by evil, and that you cannot receive any good except through eliminating the corresponding evil by realizing it and beating it back. In this view life becomes a continual combat against every imaginable form of evil, and after we have racked our brains to devise precautions against all possible evil happenings, there remains the chance, and much more than the chance, that we have by no means exhausted the category of negative possibilities, and that others may arise which no amount of foresight on our part could have imagined. The more we see into this position the more intolerable it becomes, because from this standpoint we can never attain any certain basis of action, and the forces of possible evil multiply as we contemplate them. To set forth to out-wit all evil by our own knowledge of its nature is to attempt a task the hopelessness of which becomes apparent when we see it in its true light.

The mistake is in supposing that Life can be generated in ourselves by an intellectual process; but, as we have seen in the preceding lectures, Life is the primary movement of the Spirit, whether in the cosmos or in the individual. In its proper order intellectual knowledge is exceedingly important and useful, but its place in the order of the whole is not that of the Originator. It is not Life in itself, but is a function of life; it is an effect and not the cause. The reason why this is so is because intellectual study is always the study of the various laws which arise from the different *relations* of things to one another; and it therefore presupposes that these things together with their laws are already in existence. Consequently it does not start from the truly creative standpoint, that of creating something entirely new, creation *ex nihilo* as distinguished from *construction*, or the laying-together of existing materials, which is what the word literally means. To recognize evil as a force to be reckoned with is therefore to give up the creative standpoint altogether. It is to quit the plane of First Cause and descend into the realm of secondary causation and lose ourselves amid the confusion of a multiplicity of relative causes and effects without grasping any unifying principle behind them.

Now the only thing that can release us from the inextricable confusion of an infinite multiplicity is the realization of an underlying unity, and at the back of all things we find the presence of one Great Affirmative principle without which nothing could have existence. This, then, is the Root of Life; and if we credit it with being able, not only to supply the power, but also the form for its manifestation we shall see that we need not go beyond this *single* Power for the production of anything. It is Spirit producing Substance out of its own essence, and the Substance taking Form in accordance with the movement of the

Spirit. What we have to realize is, not only that this is the way in which the cosmos is brought into existence, but also that, because the Spirit finds a new centre in ourselves, the same process is repeated in our own mentality, and therefore we are continually creating *ex nihilo* whether we know it or not. Consequently, if we look upon evil as a force to be reckoned with, and therefore requiring to be studied, we are in effect creating it; while on the other hand if we realize that there is only *one* force to be considered, and that absolutely good, we are by the law of the creative process bringing that good into manifestation. No doubt for this affirmative use of our creative power it is necessary that we start from the basic conception of a *single* originating power which is absolutely good and life-giving; but if there were a self-originating power which was destructive then no creation could ever have come into existence at all, for the positive and negative self-originating powers would cancel each other and the result would be zero. The fact, therefore, of our own existence is a sufficient proof of the singleness and goodness of the Originating Power, and from this starting point there is no second power to be taken into consideration, and consequently we do not have to study the evil that may arise out of existing or future circumstances, but require to keep our minds fixed only upon the good which we intend to create. There is a very simple reason for this. It is that every new creation necessarily carries its own law with it and by that law produces new conditions of its own. A balloon affords a familiar illustration of my meaning. The balloon with its freight weighs several hundred-weight, yet the introduction of a new factor, the gas, brings with it a law of its own which entirely alters the conditions, and the force of gravity is so completely overcome that the whole mass rises into the air. The Law itself is never altered, but we have previously known it only under limiting conditions. These conditions, however, are no part of the Law itself; and a clearer realization of the Law shows us that it contains in itself the power of transcending them. The law which every new creation carries with it is therefore not a contradiction of the old law but its specialization into a higher mode of action.

Now the ultimate Law is that of production *ex nihilo* by the movement of the Spirit within itself, and all subordinate laws are merely the measurements of the relations which spontaneously arise between different things when they are brought into manifestation, and therefore, if an entirely new thing is created it must necessarily establish entirely new relations and so produce entirely new laws. This is the reason why, if we take the action of pure unmanifested Spirit as our starting point, we may confidently trust it to produce manifestations of law which, though perfectly new from the standpoint of our past experience, are quite as natural in their own way as any that have gone before. It is on this account that in these addresses I lay so much stress on the fact that Spirit creates *ex nihilo*, that is, out of no pre-existing forms, but simply by its own movement within itself. If, then, this idea is clearly grasped, it logically follows from it that the Root of Life is not to be found in the comparison of good and evil, but in the simple affirmation of the Spirit as the All-creating power of Good. And since, as we have already seen, this same all-creating Spirit finds a centre and fresh starting point of operation in our own minds, we can trust it to follow the Law of its own being there as much as in the creation of the cosmos.

Only we must not forget that it is working through our own minds. It thinks through our mind, and our mind must be made a suitable channel for this mode of its operation by conforming itself to the broad generic lines of the Spirit's thinking. The reason for this is one which I have sought to impress throughout these lectures, namely, that the specialization of a law is never the denial of it, but on the contrary the fuller recognition of its basic principles; and if this is the case in ordinary physical science it must be equally so when we come to specialize the great Law of Life itself. The Spirit can never change its essential nature as the essence of Life, Love, and Beauty; and if we adopt these characteristics, which constitute the Law of the Spirit, as the basis of our own thinking, and reject all that is contrary to them, then we afford the broad generic conditions for the specialized thinking of the Spirit through our own minds; and the thinking of the Spirit is that *involution*, or passing of spirit into form, which is the whole being of the creative process.

The mind which is all the time being thus formed is our own. It is not a case of control by an external individuality, but the fuller expression of the Universal through an organized mentality which has all along been a less perfect expression of the Universal; and therefore the process is one of growth. We are not losing our individuality, but are coming into fuller possession of ourselves by the conscious recognition of our personal share in the great work of creation. We begin in some slight measure to understand what the Bible means when it speaks of our being "partakers of the Divine nature" (2 Peter 1:4) and we realize the significance of the "unity of the Spirit" (Ephesians 4:3). Doubtless this will imply changes in our old mode of thinking; but these changes are not forced upon us, they are brought about naturally by the new standpoint from which we now see things. Almost imperceptibly to ourselves we grow into a New Order of Thought which proceeds, not from a knowledge of good and evil, but from the Principle of Life itself. That is what makes the difference between our old thought and our new thought. Our old thought was based upon a comparison of limited facts; our new thought is based upon a comprehension of principles. The difference is like that between the mathematics of the infant, who cannot count beyond the number of apples or marbles put before him, and that of the senior wrangler who is not dependent upon visible objects for his calculations, but plunges boldly into the unknown because he knows that he is working by indubitable principles. In like manner when we realize the infallible Principle of the Creative Law we no longer find we need to see everything cut and dried beforehand, for if so, we could never get beyond the range of our old experiences; but we can move steadily forward because we know the certainty of the creative principle by which we are working, or rather, which is working through us, and that our life, in all its minutest details, is its harmonious expression. Thus the Spirit thinks through our thought only its thought is greater than ours. It is the paradox of the less containing the greater. Our thought will not be objectless or unintelligible to ourselves. It will be quite clear as far as it goes. We shall know exactly what we want to do and why we want to do it, and so will act in a reasonable and intelligent manner. But what we do not know is the greater thought that is all the time giving rise to our smaller thought, and which will open out from it as our lesser thought progresses into form. Then we gradually see the greater thought which prompted our smaller one and we find ourselves working along its lines, guided by the invisible hand of the Creative Spirit into continually increasing degrees of livingness to which we need assign no limits, for it is the expansion of the Infinite within ourselves.

This, as it appears to me, is the hidden meaning of the two trees in Eden, the Garden of the Soul. It is the distinction between a knowledge which is merely that of comparisons between different sorts of conditions, and a knowledge which is that of the Life which gives rise to and therefore controls conditions. Only we must remember that the control of conditions is not to be attained by violent self-assertion which is only recognizing them as substantive entities to be battled with, but by conscious unity with that All-creating Spirit which works silently, but surely, on its own lines of Life, Love, and Beauty.

"Not by might, nor by power, but by My Spirit, saith the Lord of Hosts."

10

THE WORSHIP OF ISHI

IN HOSEA 2:16 we find this remarkable statement: "And it shall be at that day, saith the Lord, that thou shalt call Me Ishi, and shalt no more call Me Baali"; and with this we may couple the statement in Isaiah 62:4: "Thou shalt be called Hephzibah, and thy land Beulah; for the Lord delighteth in thee, and thy land shall be married."

In both these passages we find a change of name; and since a name stands for something which corresponds to it, and in truth only amounts to a succinct description, the fact indicated in these texts is a change of condition answering to the change of name.

Now the change from Baali to Ishi indicates an important alteration in the relation between the Divine Being and the worshipper; but since the Divine Being cannot change, the altered relation must result from a change in the standpoint of the worshipper; and this can only come from a new mode of looking at the Divine, that is, from a new order of thought regarding it. Baali means Lord, and Ishi means husband, and so the change in relation is that of a female slave who is liberated and married to her former master. We could not have a more perfect analogy. Relatively to the Universal Spirit the individual soul is esoterically feminine, as I have pointed out in *Bible Mystery and Bible Meaning*, because its function is that of the receptive and formative. This is necessarily inherent in the nature of the creative process. But the individual's development as the specializing medium of the Universal Spirit will depend entirely upon his own conception of his relation to it. So long as he only regards it as an arbitrary power, a sort of slave-owner, he will find himself in the position of a slave driven by an inscrutable force, he knows not whither or for what purpose. He may worship such a God, but his worship is only the worship of fear and ignorance, and there is no personal interest in the matter except to escape some dreaded punishment. Such a worshipper would gladly escape from his divinity, and his worship, when analyzed, will be found to be little else than disguised hatred. This is the natural result of a worship based upon *unexplained* traditions instead of intelligible principles, and is the very opposite of that worship in Spirit and in truth which Jesus speaks of as the true worship.

But when the light begins to break in upon us, all this becomes changed. We see that a system of terrorism cannot give expression to the Divine Spirit, and we realize the truth of St. Paul's words, "He hath not given us the spirit of fear, but of power, and of love, and of a sound mind." As the true nature of the relation between the individual mind and the Universal Mind becomes clearer, we find it to be one of mutual action and reaction, a perfect reciprocity which cannot be better symbolized than by the relation between an affectionate husband and wife. Everything is done from love and nothing from compulsion, there is perfect confidence on both sides, and both are equally indispensable to each other. It is simply the carrying out of the fundamental maxim that the Universal cannot act on the plane of the Particular except through the Particular; only this philosophical axiom develops into a warm living intercourse.

Now this is the position of the soul which is indicated by the name Hephzibah. In common with all other words derived from the Semitic root "hafz" it implies the idea of guarding, just as in the East a *hafiz* is one who guards the letter of the Koran by having the whole book by heart, and in many similar expressions. Hephzibah may therefore be translated as "a guarded one," thus recalling the New Testament description of those who are "guarded into salvation." It is precisely this conception of being guarded by a superior power that distinguishes the worship of Ishi from that of Baali. A special relation has been established between the Divine Spirit and the individual soul, one of absolute confidence and personal intercourse. This does not require any departure from the general law of the universe, but is due to that specializing of the law through the presentation of special conditions personal to the individual, of which I have spoken before. But all the time there has been no change in the Universal Spirit, the only change has been in the mental attitude of the individual—he has come into a new thought, a clearer perception of God. He has faced the questions, What is God? Where is

God? How does God work? and he has found the answer in the apostolic statement that God is "over all, through all, and in all," and he realises that "God" is the root of his (the individual's) own being, ever present *in* him, ever working *through* him, and universally present around him.

This realization of the true relation between the Originating Spirit and the individual mind is what is esoterically spoken of as the Mystical Marriage in which the two have ceased to be separate and have become one. As a matter of fact they always were one, but since we can apprehend things only from the standpoint of our own consciousness, it is our recognition of the fact that makes it a practical reality for ourselves. But an intelligent recognition will never make a confusion of the two parts of which the whole consists, and will never lead the individual to suppose that he is handling a blind force or that a blind force is handling him. He will neither dethrone God, nor lose himself by absorption in deity, but he will recognize the reciprocity of the Divine and the human as the natural and logical outcome of the essential conditions of the creative process.

And what is the Whole which is thus created? It is our conscious *personality*; and therefore whatever we draw from the Universal Spirit acquires in us the quality of personality. It is that process of differentiation of the universal into the particular of which I have so often spoken, which, by a rude analogy, we may compare to the differentiation of the universal electric fluid into specific sorts of power by its passage through suitable apparatus. It is for this reason that relatively to ourselves the Universal Spirit must necessarily assume a personal aspect, and that the aspect which it will assume will be in exact correspondence with our own conception of it. This is in accordance with mental and spiritual laws inherent in our own being, and it is on this account that the Bible seeks to build up our conception of God on such lines as will set us free from all fear of evil, and thus leave us at liberty to use the creative power of our thought affirmatively from the standpoint of a calm and untroubled mind. This standpoint can only be reached by passing beyond the range of the happenings of the moment, and this can only be done by the discovery of our immediate relation to the undifferentiated source of all good. I lay stress on these words "immediate" and "undifferentiated" because in them is contained the secret of the whole position. If we could not draw immediately from the Universal Spirit our receiving would be subject to the limitations of the channel through which it reached us; and if the force which we receive were not undifferentiated in itself it could not take appropriate form in our own minds and become to each of us just what we require it to be. It is this power of the human soul to differentiate limitlessly from the Infinite that we are apt to overlook, but as we come to realize that the soul is itself a reflection and image of the Infinite Spirit—and a clear recognition of the cosmic creative process shows that it cannot be anything else—we find that it must possess this power, and that in fact it is our possession of this power which is the whole *raison d'être* of the creative process; if the human soul did not possess an unlimited power of differentiation from the Infinite, then the Infinite would not be reflected in it, and consequently the Infinite Spirit would find no outlet for its *conscious* recognition of itself as the Life, Love, and Beauty which it is. We can never too deeply ponder the old esoteric definition of Spirit as "the Power which knows itself"; the secret of all things, past, present, and future is contained in these few words. The self-recognition or self-contemplation of Spirit is the primary movement out of which all creation proceeds, and the attainment in the individual of a fresh centre for self-recognition is what the Spirit *gains* in the process—this *gain* accruing to the Spirit is what is referred to in the parables where the lord is represented as receiving increase from his servants.

When the individual perceives this relation between himself and Infinite Spirit, he finds that he has been raised from a position of slavery to one of reciprocity. The Spirit cannot do without him any more than he can do without the Spirit; the two are as necessary to each other as the two poles of an electric battery. The Spirit is the unlimited essence of Love, Wisdom, and Power, all three in one undifferentiated and waiting to be differentiated by *appropriation*, that is, by the individual *claiming* to be the channel of their differentiation. It only requires the claim to be made with the recognition that by the Law of Being it is bound to be answered, and the right feeling, the right seeing, and the right working for the particular matter we have in hand will flow in quite naturally. Our old enemies, doubt and fear, may seek to bring us back under bondage to Baali, but our new standpoint for the recognition of the All-originating Spirit as being absolutely unified with ourselves must always be kept resolutely in mind; for, short of this, we are not working on the creative level—we are creating, indeed, for we can never divest ourselves of our creative power, but we are creating in the image of the old limiting and destructive conditions, and this is merely perpetuating the cosmic Law of Averages, which is just what the individual has to rise superior to. The creative level is where new laws begin to manifest themselves in a new order of conditions, something transcending our past experiences and thus bringing about a real advance; for it is no advance only to go on in the same old round even if we kept at it for centuries; it is the steady go-ahead nature of the Spirit that has made the world of today an improvement upon the world of the pterodactyl and the icthyosaurus, and we must look for the same forward movement of the Spirit from its new starting point in ourselves.

Now it is this special, personal, and individual relation of the Spirit to ourselves which is typified by the names Ishi and Hephzibah. From this standpoint we may say that as the individual wakes up to the oneness with the Spirit, the Spirit wakes up to the same thing. It becomes conscious of itself through the consciousness of the individual, and thus is solved the paradox of individual self-recognition by the Universal Spirit, without which no *new*-creative power could be exercised and all things would continue to proceed in the old merely cosmic order. It is of course true that in the merely generic order the Spirit must be present in every form of Life, as the Master pointed out when He said that not a sparrow falls to the ground without "the Father." But as the sparrows He alluded to had been shot and were on sale at a price which shows that this was the fate of a good many of them, we see here precisely that stage of manifestation where the Spirit has not woke up to individual self-recognition, and remains at the lower level of self-recognition, that of the generic or race-spirit. The Master's comment, "Ye are of more value than many sparrows," points out this difference; in us the generic creation has reached the level which affords the conditions for the waking up of the Spirit to self-recognition in the Individual.

And we must bear in mind that all this is perfectly natural. There is no posing or straining after effect about it. If *you* have to pump up the Life, who is going to put the Life into you to pump it? Therefore it is spontaneous or nothing. That is why the Bible speaks of it as the free gift of God. It cannot be anything else. You cannot originate the originating force; it must originate you; but what you can do is to distribute it. Therefore immediately you experience any sense of friction be sure there is something wrong somewhere; and since God can never change, you may be sure that the friction is being caused by some error in your own thinking—you are limiting the Spirit in some way; set to work to find out what it is. It is always *limiting* the Spirit that does this. You are tying it down to conditions somewhere, saying it is bound by reason of some existing forms. The remedy is to go back to the original starting point of the Cosmic Creation and ask, Where were the pre-existing forms that dictated to the Spirit then? Then because the Spirit never changes it is *still the same*, and is just as independent of existing conditions now as it was in the beginning; and so we must pass over all existing conditions, however apparently adverse, and go straight to the Spirit as the originator of new forms and new conditions. This is real New Thought, for it does not trouble about the old things, but is going straight ahead from where we are now. When we do this, just trusting the Spirit, and not laying down the particular details of its action—just telling it what we want without dictating *how* we are to get it—we shall find that things will open out more and more clearly day by day both on the inner and the outer plane. Remember that the Spirit is alive and working here and now, for if ever the Spirit is to get from the past into the future it must be by passing through the present; therefore what you have to do is to acquire the habit of living direct from the Spirit here and now. You will soon find that this is a matter of personal intercourse, perfectly natural and not requiring any abnormal conditions for its production. You just treat the Spirit as you would any other kind-hearted sensible person, remembering that it is always there—"closer than hands and feet," as Tennyson says—and you will gradually begin to appreciate its reciprocity as a very practical fact indeed.

This is the relation of Hephzibah to Ishi, and is that worship in Spirit and in truth which needs neither the temple in Jerusalem nor yet in Samaria for its acceptance, for the whole world is the temple of the Spirit and you yourself its sanctuary. Bear this in mind, and remember that nothing is too great or too small, too interior or too external, for the Spirit's recognition and operation, for the Spirit is itself both the Life and the Substance of all things and it is also Self-recognition from the standpoint of your own individuality; and therefore, because the Self-recognition of Spirit is the Life of the creative process, you will, by simply trusting the Spirit to work according to its own nature, pass more and more completely into that New Order which proceeds from the thought of Him who says, "Behold I make all things new."

11

THE SHEPHERD AND THE STONE

THE METAPHOR of the Shepherd and the Sheep is of constant occurrence throughout the Bible and naturally suggests the idea of the guiding, guarding, and feeding both of the individual sheep and of the whole flock and it is not difficult to see the spiritual correspondence of these things in a general sort of way. But we find that the Bible combines the metaphor of the Shepherd with another metaphor, that of "the Stone," and at first sight the two seem rather incongruous.

"From thence is the Shepherd the Stone of Israel," says the Old Testament (Genesis 49:24), and Jesus calls himself both "The Good Shepherd" and "The Stone which the builders rejected." The Shepherd and the Stone are thus identified and we must therefore seek the interpretation in some conception which combines the two. A shepherd suggests Personal care for the welfare of the sheep, and an intelligence greater than theirs. A stone suggests the idea of Building, and consequently of measurement, adaptation of parts to whole, and progressive construction according to plan. Combining these two conceptions we get the idea of the building of an edifice whose stones are persons, each taking their more or less conscious part in the construction—thus a building, not constructed from without, but self-forming by a principle of growth from within under the guidance of a Supreme Wisdom permeating the whole and conducting it stage by stage to ultimate completeness. This points to a Divine Order in human affairs with which we may more or less consciously cooperate—both to our personal advantage and also to the furtherance of the great scheme of human evolution as a whole; the ultimate purpose being to establish in *all* men that principle of "The Octave" to which I have already alluded; and in proportion as some adumbration of this principle is realized by individuals and by groups of individuals they specialize the law of race-development, even though they may not be aware of the fact, and so come under a *specialized* working of the fundamental Law, which thus differentiates them from other individuals and nationalities, as by a peculiar guidance, producing higher developments which the merely generic operation of the Law could not.

Now if we keep steadily in mind that, though the purpose, or Law of Tendency, of the Originating Spirit must always be universal in its nature, it must necessarily be individual in its operation, we shall see that this universal purpose can only be accomplished through the instrumentality of specific means. This results from the fundamental proposition that the Universal can only work on the plane of the Particular by becoming the individual and particular; and when we grasp the conception that the merely generic operation of the Creative Law has now brought the human race as far as it can, that is to say it has completely evolved the merely natural *genus homo*, it follows that if any further development is to take place it can only be by the cooperation of the individual himself. Now it is the spread of this individual cooperation that the forward movement of the Spirit is leading us to, and it is the gradual extension of this universal principle that is alluded to in the prophecy of Daniel regarding the Stone cut out without hands that spreads until it fills the whole earth (Daniel 2:34 and 44). According to the interpretation given by Daniel, this Stone is the emblem of a spiritual Kingdom, and the identity of the Stone and the Shepherd indicates that the Kingdom of the Stone must be also the Kingdom of the Shepherd; and the Master, who identified himself with both the Stone and the Shepherd, emphatically declared that this Kingdom was, in its essence, an interior Kingdom—"the Kingdom of Heaven is within you." We must look for its foundation therefore in a spiritual principle or mental law inherent in the constitution of all men but waiting to be brought into fuller development by more accurate compliance with its essential requirements; which is precisely the method by which science has evoked powers from the laws of nature which were undreamt of in former ages; and in like manner the recognition of our true relation to the Universal Spirit, which is the source of all individual being, must lead to an advance both for the race and for the individual such as we can at present scarcely form the faintest idea of, but which we dimly apprehend through the intuition and speak of as the New Order. The approach of this New Order is everywhere making itself vaguely felt; it is, as the French say, in the air, and the very vagueness and mystery attending it is causing a feeling of unrest as to what form it may assume. But to the student of Spiritual Law this should not be the case. He knows that the Form is always the expression of the Spirit, and therefore, since he is in touch with the forward movement of the Spirit, he knows that he himself will always be harmoniously included in any form of development which the Great Forward Movement may take. This is the practical and personal benefit arising from the realization of the Principle which is symbolized under the twofold metaphor of the Shepherd and the Stone, and in all those new developments which are perhaps even now within measurable distance, we can rest on the knowledge that we are under the care of a kind Shepherd, and under the formation of a wise Master Builder.

But the principle of the Shepherd and the Stone is not something hitherto unheard of which is only to come into existence in the future. If there were no manifestations of this principle in the past, we might question whether there were any such principle at all; but a careful study of the subject will show us that it has been at work all through the ages, sometimes in modes more immediately bearing the aspect of the Shepherd, and sometimes in modes more immediately bearing the aspect of the Stone, though the one always implies the other, for they are the same thing seen from different points of view. The subject is one of immense interest, but covering such a wide range of study that all I can do here is to point out that such a field of investigation exists and is worth exploration; and the exploration brings its reward with it, not only by putting us in possession of the key to the history of the past, but by showing us that it is the key to the history of the future also, and furthermore by making evident on a large scale the working of the same principle of Spiritual Law by cooperation with which we may facilitate the process of our own individual evolution. It thus adds a vivid interest to life, giving us something worth looking forward to and introducing us to a personal future which is not limited by the proverbial threescore years and ten.

Now, we have seen that the first stage in the Creative Process is always that of Feeling—a reaching-out by the Spirit in a particular direction, and therefore we may look for something of the same kind in the development of the great principle which we are now considering. And we find this first vague movement of this great principle in the intuitions of a particular race which appears from time immemorial to have combined the two characteristics of nomad wandering with their flocks and herds and the symbolization of their religious beliefs in monuments of stone. The monuments themselves have taken different forms in different countries and ages, but the identity of their symbolism becomes clear under careful investigation. Together with this symbolism we always find the nomad character of the builders and that they are invested with an aura of mystery and romance such as we find nowhere else, though we always find it surrounding these builders, even in countries so far apart as India and Ireland. Then, as we pass beyond the merely monumental stage, we find threads of historical evidence connecting the different branches of this race, increasing in their complexity and strengthening in their cumulative force as we go on, until at last we are brought to the history of the age in which we live; and finally most remarkable affinities of language put the finishing touch to the mass of proofs which can be gathered along all these different lines. In this magic circle countries so remote from one another as Ireland and Greece, Egypt and India, Palestine and Persia, are brought into close contiguity—a similar tradition, and even a similar nomenclature, unite the mysterious builders of the Great Pyramid with the equally mysterious builders of the Round Towers of Ireland—and the Great Pyramid itself, perhaps antedating the call of Abraham, reappears as the official seal of the United States; while tradition traces the crowning-stone in Westminster Abbey back to the time of Solomon's temple and even earlier. For the most part the erewhile wanderers are now settled in their destined homes, but the Anglo-Saxon race—the People of the Corner-Stone—are still the pioneers among the nations, and there is something esoteric in the old joke that when the North Pole is reached a Scotchman will be found there. And not least in the chain of evidence is the link afforded by a tribe who are wanderers still, the Gypsies with their duplicate of the Pyramid in the pack of cards—a volume which has been called "The Devil's Picture Book" by those who know it only in its misuse and inversion, but which when interpreted in the light of the knowledge we are now gaining, affords a signal instance of that divine policy by which as St. Paul says, God employs the foolish things of this world to confute the wise; while a truer apprehension of the Gypsies themselves indicates their unmistakable connection with that race who through all its wanderings has ever been the guardian of the Stone.

In these few paragraphs I have only been able to point out very briefly the broad lines of enquiry into a subject of national importance to the British and American peoples, and which interests us personally, not only as members of these nations, but as affording proof on the largest scale of the same specialization of universal laws which each of us has to effect individually for ourself. But whether the process be individual or national it is always the same, and is the translation to the very highest plane—that of the All-originating Life itself—of the old maxim that "Nature will obey us exactly in proportion as we first obey Nature"; it is the old parable of the lord who, finding his servants girt and awaiting him, then girds himself and serves them (Luke 12:35-37). The nation or the individual who thus realizes the true principle of the Shepherd and the Stone, comes under a special Divine guidance and protection, not by a favouritism incompatible with the conception of universal Law, but by the very operation of the Law itself. They have come into touch with its higher possibilities, and to recur to an analogy which I have already employed, they learn to make their iron float by the very same law by which it sinks; and so they become the flock of the Great Shepherd and the building of the Great Architect, and each one, however insignificant his or her sphere may appear, becomes a sharer in the great work, and by a logical consequence begins to grow on new lines of development for the simple reason that a new principle necessarily produces new modes of manifestation. If the reader will think over these things he will see that the promises contained in the Bible, whether national or personal, are nothing else than statements of the universal law of Cause and Effect applied to the inmost principles of our being, and that therefore it is not mere rhapsody, but the figurative expression of a great truth when the Psalmist says "The Lord is my Shepherd," and "Thou art my God and the Rock of my salvation."

12

SALVATION IS OF THE JEWS

WHAT DOES THIS saying of the Master's mean? Certainly not a mere arrogant assumption in favour of His own nationality—such an idea is negatived, not only by the universality of all His other teaching, but also by the very instruction in which these words occur, for He declared that the Jewish temple was equally with the Samaritan of no account in the matter. He said that the true worship was purely spiritual and entirely independent of places and ceremonies, while at the same time He emphasized the Jewish expectation of a Messiah, so that in this teaching we are met by the paradox of a universal principle combined with what at first sight appears like a tribal tradition quite incompatible with any recognition of the universal reign of law. How to reconcile these apparent opposites, therefore, seems to be the problem which He here sets before us. Its solution is to be found in that principle which I have endeavoured to elucidate throughout these lectures, the specializing of universal law. Opinions may differ as to whether the Bible narrative of the birth of Christ is to be taken literally or symbolically, but as to the spiritual principle involved there can, I think, be no difference of opinion. It is that of the specialization by the individual of the generic relation of the soul to the Infinite Spirit from which it proceeds. The relation itself is universal and results from the very nature of the creative process, but the law of the universal relation admits of particular specialization exactly in the same way as all other natural laws—it is simply applying to the supreme Law of Life the same method by which we have learnt to make iron float, that is to say by a fuller recognition of what the Law is in itself. Whatever other meanings we may apply to the name Messiah, it undoubtedly stands for the absolutely perfect manifestation in the individual of all the infinite possibilities of the Principle of Life.

Now it was because this grand ideal is the basis on which the Hebrew nationality was founded that Jesus made this statement. This foundation had been lamentably misconceived by the Jewish people; but nevertheless, however imperfectly, they still held by it, and from them this ideal has spread throughout the Christian world. Here also it continues to be lamentably misconceived, nevertheless it is still retained, and only needs to be recognized in its true light as a universal principle, instead of an unintelligible dogma, to become the salvation of the world. Hence, as affording the medium through which this supreme ideal has been preserved and spread, it is true that "Salvation is of the Jews."

Their fundamental idea was right but their apprehension of it was wrong—that is why the Master at the same time sweeps away the national worship of the temple and preserves the national idea of the Messiah; and this is equally true of the Christian world at the present day. If salvation is anything real it must have its cause in some law, and if there is a law it must be founded upon some universal principle; therefore it is this principle which we must seek if we would understand this teaching of the Master's.

Now whether we take the Bible story of the birth of Christ literally or symbolically, it teaches one great lesson. It teaches that the All-originating Spirit is the true Parent of the individual both in soul and body. This is nothing else than realizing from the standpoint of the individual what we cannot help realizing in regard to the original creation of the cosmos—it is the realization that the All-originating Spirit is at once the Life and the Substance in each individual here and now, just as it must have been in the origin of all things. Human parentage counts for nothing—it is only the channel through which Universal Spirit has acted for the concentration of an individual centre; but the ultimate cause of that centre, both in life and substance, continues at every moment to be the One same Originating Spirit.

This recognition cuts away the root of all the power of the negative, and so in principle it delivers us from all evil, for the root of evil is the denial of the power of the Spirit to produce good. When we realize that the Spirit is finding its own individualization in us in its twofold essence as Life and Substance, then we see that it must be both able and willing to create for us all good. The only limit is that which we ourselves impose by denying its operation, and when we realize the inherent creativeness of Spirit we find that there is no reason why we should stop short at any point and say that it can go no further. Our error is in looking on the life of the body as separate from the life of the

Spirit, and this error is met by the consideration that, in its ultimate nature, Substance must emanate from Spirit and is nothing else than the record of Spirit's conception of itself as finding expression in space and time. And when this becomes clear it follows that Substance need not be taken into calculation at all. The material form stands in the same relation to Spirit that the image projected on the screen stands to the slide in the lantern. If we wish to change the exhibited subject we do not manipulate the reflection on the screen, but we alter the slide; and in like manner, when we come to realize the true nature of the creative process, we learn that the exterior things are to be changed by a change of the interior spiritual attitude. Our spiritual attitude will always be determined by our conception of our relation to God or Infinite Spirit; and so when we begin to see that this relation is one of absolute reciprocity—that it is the self-recognition of Infinite Spirit from our own centre of consciousness—then we find that the whole Secret of Life consists in simple reliance upon the All-creating Spirit as consciously identifying itself with us. It has, so to say, awakened to a new mode of self-recognition peculiar to ourselves, in which we individually form the centre of its creative energy. To realize this is to specialize the Principle of Life. The logic of it is simple. We have found that the originating movement of Spirit from which all creation proceeds can only be Self-contemplation. Then, since the Original Spirit cannot change its nature, its self-contemplation through our own minds must be as creative in, for, and through us as it ever was in the beginning; and consequently we find the original creative process repeated in ourselves and directed by the conscious thought of our own minds.

In all this there is no place for the consideration of outward conditions, whether of body or circumstances; for they are only effects and not the cause; and therefore when we reach this standpoint we cease to take them into our calculations. Instead we employ the method of self-contemplation, knowing that this is the creative method, and so we contemplate ourselves as allied to the infinite Love and Wisdom of the Divine Spirit which will take form through our conscious thought, and so act creatively as a Special Providence entirely devoted to guarding, guiding, providing for, and illuminating us. The whole thing is perfectly natural when seen from a clear recognition of what the creative working of Spirit must be in itself; and when it is realized in this perfectly natural manner all strain and effort to compel its action ceases—we are at one with the All-creating Power which has now found a new centre in ourselves from which to continue its creative work to more perfect manifestation than could be attained through the unspecialized generic conditions of the merely cosmic order.

Now this is what Messiah stands for, and therefore it is written that "to them gave He power to become sones of God, even to as many as believe on His Name." This "belief" is the recognition of a universal principle and personal reliance upon it as a law which cannot be broken; for it is the Law of the whole creative process specialized in our own individuality. Then, too, however great may be the mystery, the removal and cleansing away of all sin follows as an essential part of this realization of new life; and it is in this sense that we may read all that the Bible tells us on this aspect of the subject. The *principle* of it is

Love; for when we are reunited to the Parent Spirit in mutual confidence and love, what room is there on either side for any remembrance of our past failures?

This, then, is what Messiah stands for to the individual; but if we can conceive a nation based upon such a recognition of its special relation to the Directing Power of the Universe, such a people must of necessity become the leader of the nations, and those who oppose it must fail by a self-destructive principle inherent in the very nature of the position they take up. The leadership resulting from such a national self-recognition, will not be based upon conquest and compulsion, but will come naturally. Other nations will enquire the reason for the phenomenal success and prosperity of the favoured people, and finding this reason in a universal Law, they will begin to apply the same law in the same manner, and thus the same results will spread from country to country until at last the whole earth will be full of the glory of the Lord. And such a nation, and rather company of nations, exists. To trace its present development from its ancient beginnings is far beyond the scope of this volume, and still more to speculate upon its further growth; but to my readers on both sides of the Atlantic I may say that this people is the Anglo-Saxon race throughout the world. I write these lines upon the historic Hill of Tara; this will convey a hint to many of my readers. At some further time I may enlarge upon this subject; but at present my aim is merely to suggest some lines of thought arising from the Master's saying that "Salvation is of the Jews."

NOTES

It is hoped that the following notes, keyed to pages and lines of this book, will provide helpful references to texts cited by the author as well as clarify some matters that might otherwise be obscure.

A.V.

PAGE	LINE(S)	
8	22-23	The lines are from Tennyson's *In Memoriam*. The serious student will want to consult *The Law of Psychic Phenomena*, chapter 2, by Thomson Jay Hudson (1893) for the source of Troward's illumination on this subject.
19	21	*a priori* reasoning: reasoning from self-evident propositions.
21	2-3	syllogism: logical deduction of a third proposition (the conclusion) from two preceding ones (the premises). Ex.: (1) All girls are female. (2) Mary is a girl. (3) Therefore Mary is a female.
34	3	(Sir) J(ohn) A(mbrose) Fleming, English electrical engineer.
38	25	the apostolic words: Hebrews 11:1.
40	27-29	"He that . . . not hear?": Psalm 94:9.
42	22	Via Dolorosa ("sorrowful way"): the route along which Jesus carried his cross.
43	6, 7	Jachin and Boaz: the twin pillars at the entrance to Solomon's temple (2 Chron. 3:17), symbolic of the subjective and objective forces respectively. "The combined action of Law [Jachin] and Volition [or Personality; Boaz], . . . they contain the key to the entire Bible and to the whole order of Nature . . . emblems of the two great principles of the

		universe." See *Collected Essays of Thomas Troward*, "Jachin and Boaz" (pp. 150-53), and chapter 6 of his *Bible Mystery and Bible Meaning*.
45	21	"Ye know all things": 1 John 2:20.
49	22	*Quot homines tot sententiæ*: "There are as many opinions as there are persons."
56	22-23	*ad infinitum*: "to infinity."
63	7	*en rapport*: "in relation [keeping, harmony]" (with).
68	24	from the *plenum* to the *vacuum*: here, in the sense "from the fulness to the emptiness."
76	13-14	*in extenso*: "at full length."
84	6	*a fortiori*: in the sense "with still greater reason," "all the more so."
90	26-28	Ask and . . . unto you: see Matthew 7:7, Luke 11:9.
104	4	Oriental systems: this refers to the "awakening" or raising of the so-called Kundalini power upward through spinal centers called chakras.
111	16	R.C.: *Rosæ Crucis* ("of the Rosy Cross").
	17-18	books M. and T.: (1) Book M, *Liber Mundi* ("Book of the World"), is understood by some to refer metaphorically to the "Book of Life," "Book of Nature," etc. (2) The initial Rosicrucian manifesto, *Fama Fraternitatis*, refers to "a parchment called T, the which next unto the Bible is our greatest treasure." Paul Foster Case says that Book T is a symbol, and he uses the Cabalah to equate it with the book described in Revelation 5:1 as being sealed with seven seals, concluding that this in turn is "simply the human body, and its seals are the force-centers wherein radiates the formative force of the Logos," the seals thereby representing the system of chakras. "Thus we may understand Book T to be the record of all time, written on the

flesh of the human body, within and without."

24 *Jesus mihi omnia*: literally, "Jesus is all things to me"—the Rosicrucian motto. Paul Foster Case writes, "The name Jesus signifies 'Self-existence liberates.'" Connected with *omnia* ("all things"), this "intimates the characteristic Rosicrucian point of view, which is that everything contributes to liberation. . . . Thus the motto is the affirmation of the inherent tendency to liberty, as the very heart of the cosmic order." This theme recurs constantly in Troward's works.

25-26 "the Artist Elias"; the Magnum Opus: "the Artist Elias" is significant of the "Great Work" (*Magnum Opus*) of self-liberation to be accomplished by the individual. The biblical symbolism combines reference to the "Great Art" of the Rosicrucians with the prophet Elias, of whom it is said that he shall return and "restore all things" (Matt. 17:11). The Great Art—equivalent of the Great Work of the Hermetic philosophers—is, according to Paul Foster Case, the work of those who know "the secret of regeneration. Thus they can use the law that has evolved man out of the lower kingdoms to take man farther, out of the limitations of his natural state."

Elias, figured as returning to restore all things, is emblematic of renewal and of the Great Art, or Great Work, itself. Significantly, Jesus is represented as saying (Matt. 17:12) that "Elias is come already." This wrests the reference from its strictly temporal context and makes it applicable to the individual of any time and place. The relevance of all this to Troward's message will readily suggest itself to the reader of his works.

For an excellent account and study of

Page	Line	Note
		Rosicrucianism largely consistent with Troward's teachings and occasionally citing his texts, see Paul Foster Case, *The True and Invisible Rosicrucian Order* (York Beach, Maine: Samuel Weiser, Inc., 1985), from which the above quotations are taken.
117	Title	See *Collected Essays of Thomas Troward*, "Entering into the Spirit of It," (pp. 45-49).
119	31	*fons et origo*: "fountain and origin."
123	18	*de novo*: "anew."
136	18	*causa causans*: "cause [as] causing"; *causa causata*: "cause [as] caused."
137-38	31-9	This is the only treatment by Troward to appear in print.
138	7	"it will move forward": in teaching from *The Doré Lectures,* Raymond Charles Barker would have his students amend this to read, "it now moves forward," in order to secure a present, and not a deferred, demonstration. In *The Science of Mind* Ernest Holmes writes, "If we say, 'Tomorrow it is going to be,' then according to the very law we are using we hold the answer in a state of futurity which can never become present" (p. 289).
146-47	32-1	"Despise not the day of small things": based on Zechariah 4:10.
149	Title	Alpha (A) and Omega (Ω) are the first and last letters respectively of the Greek alphabet (see Rev. 1:11).
150	7-8	"Like unto a son of man": Revelation 1:13.
	32	*ab initio*: "from the beginning."
152	29-30	"renewed in knowledge": Colossians 3:10.
153	21	*ex nihilo*: "out of nothing."
155	15	*Quoad*: "as," "in the capacity of."
159	21-23	"Seek ye . . . unto you": Matthew 6:33; Luke 12:31.
164	17	"I and my Father are ONE": John 10:30.

170 14-15 the process by which the Yod of Yod becomes the Yod of He: Yod (the tenth letter of the Hebrew alphabet and "structurally" the foundation of all the others), Troward tells us elsewhere, is "a symbol of the all-originating First Principle." He (the fifth letter) "indicates that which is not self-contained, but which emanates from the Source of Life. Yod thus represents Essential Life, while He represents Derived Life." See his *Bible Mystery and Bible Meaning*, ch. 7, "The Sacred Name." Yod is the first letter of the Tetragrammaton (the Divine Name—IHVH), the "paternal" letter, and thus suggests masculinity, the Father. He, the second letter of the Tetragrammaton and in a sense representative of the remaining letters, is called "the Mother wherewith creation took place." Paul Foster Case says that He "conceals the paternal Yod," "conceals the Word," because "the value of the letter name [twice 5] is 10, [which is the numerical value of Yod and] which reduces to 1, the number of Aleph, and Aleph stands for the Creative Word (the Divine Name, IHVH) which calls all things into being." See pp. 50-61 (He) and pp. 98-103 (Yod) of Case's *The Book of Tokens: Tarot Meditations* (Los Angeles: Builders of the Adytum, 1934). "The process by which the Yod of Yod becomes the Yod of He" is therefore the same process by which "the Octave is the starting point of a new series reduplicating the starting point of the previous series at a different level, [and] the second series comes out of the first by natural growth and could not come into existence without it. . . . " (*Doré Lectures*, pp. 169, 170).

175 7 Origen: ca. A.D. 185-254; Greek writer, teacher, and Church father.

182 28-29 "Not by . . . of Hosts": Zechariah 4:6.

184	27-29	"He hath . . . sound mind": 2 Timothy 1:7.
185	18	"guarded into salvation": possibly a reference to 1 Peter 1:5.
186	2-3	"over all, through all, and in all": Ephesians 4:6.
187	31	*raison d'être*: "reason for being."
192	9-10	"Behold I make all things new": Revelation 21:5.
193	13	"The Good Shepherd": John 10:14.
	13-14	"The Stone which the builders rejected": Luke 20:17.
195	2	*genus homo*: the (biological) "classification: man."
198	11-12	the official seal of the United States: See Paul Foster Case, *The Great Seal of the United States: Its History, Symbolism and Message for the New Age* (Los Angeles: Builders of the Adytum, 1935), and Emmet Fox, *The Historical Destiny of the United States: The Mystery of the American Money* (DeVorss & Co.; also appears in Fox's *Alter Your Life*).
200	4-5	"The Lord is my Shepherd": Psalm 23:1.
	5-6	"Thou art . . . my salvation": Psalm 89:26.
201	Title	John 4:22.
205	24-26	"to them . . . His Name": John 1:12.
206	26-27	"the historic Hill of Tara": seat of the ancient Irish kings. See p. 198, lines 3-10.